Stylish, picture-perfect and delicious, macarons are the ultimate in pretty sweet treats. Adaptable to any colour scheme or flavouring, these delicate little fancies make the perfect gift or centerpiece for a smart afternoon tea.

This gorgeous book gives you step-by-step instructions on how to master the basic macaron technique so that you always get a crisp exterior, chewy cookie, and flavoursome filling. Recipes to ~~~~~~~~~~ ramel, pistachio, lemon, ~~~~~~~~~~~ nd chocolate, malted milk ~~~~~~~~~~~ erry and passion fruit. ~~~~~~~~~~ you can try your hand at the ~~~~~~~~~~~ decorated macarons, from cute pandas to flowers, caterpillars to Chinese lanterns, bumble bees to tennis balls, these stunning and playful designs are guaranteed to delight and thrill.

Macarons

65 recipes for chic & delicious treats

Annie Rigg & Loretta Liu

RYLAND PETERS & SMALL
LONDON • NEW YORK

ISBN: 978-1-78879-201-1

A CIP record for this book is available from the
British Library. A CIP record for this book is
available from the Library of Congress

Printed in China

Senior Designer Sonya Nathoo
Production Manager Gordana Simakovic
Art Director Leslie Harrington
Editorial Director Julia Charles
Publisher Cindy Richards
Indexer Vanessa Bird

First published in 2020
by Ryland Peters & Small
20–21 Jockey's Fields
London WC1R 4BW
and
341 East 116th Street,
New York, NY 10029

www.rylandpeters.com

10 9 8 7 6 5 4 3 2 1

Important Notes
• The recipes in the Decorated Macarons section
of this book (pages 76–139) use Sugarflair food
colouring pastes (not liquids) so the colours refer
to an exact shade. If you use a different brand of
paste, Loretta suggests you use the photographs
in the book to match the colours she has chosen.
See page 144 for a list of recommended suppliers.
• Both British (Metric) and American (Imperial
plus US cups) are included in these recipes. It is
important to work with one set of measurements
and not alternate between the two within a recipe.
• All spoon measurements are level unless otherwise
specified; a tablespoon is 15 ml, a teaspoon is 5 ml.
• Eggs used in this book are (UK) medium and (US)
large unless otherwise stated.
• Ovens should always be preheated to the specified
temperature before baking.

Contents

Making macarons

Basic macarons

This basic macaron recipe is ideal for the beginner. Use it to make all the Classic Macaron recipes on pages 32–75, or simply make the shells in any of the Classic Flavour Variations (see pages 8–9) and fill them with the quick fillings (see page 26) or homemade fillings (see pages 27–31) or your choice.

200 g/1½ cups icing/confectioners' sugar
100 g/⅔ cup ground almonds
120–125 g/½ cup egg whites (about 3 eggs)
a pinch of salt
40 g/3 tablespoons caster/superfine sugar

a 5-cm/1-inch cookie cutter (optional)
2 heavy baking sheets, lined with baking parchment
a hand-held electric whisk
a rubber spatula
piping bag, fitted with a 1-cm/½-inch tip

MAKES ABOUT 40 5-CM/2-INCH SHELLS

PREPARATION: Draw 20 circles around the cookie cutter on a baking parchment sheet and turn it over. You will be piping the macaron mixture onto each circle. Set aside until needed. Note: If you are using a fan oven, you might consider using the silicone mat method given in the Patissier's Macaron recipe (see page 10), as the sheets of baking parchment can blow around the oven and spoil the macarons.

1. Tip the icing/confectioners' sugar and almonds into the bowl of a food processor and blend for 30 seconds until thoroughly combined. Set aside.

2. Tip the egg whites into a spotlessly clean and dry mixing bowl. Add the salt and, using an electric hand-held whisk, beat until they will only just hold a stiff peak.

3. Continue to whisk at medium speed while adding the caster/superfine sugar a teaspoonful at a time. Mix well between each addition to ensure that the sugar is thoroughly incorporated before adding the next spoonful. The mixture should be thick, white and glossy.

4. At this point you should add any food colouring you are using. Dip a cocktail stick into the food colouring paste and stir into the mixture, mixing thoroughly to ensure that the colour is evenly blended. Scrape down the sides of the bowl with a rubber spatula.

5. Using a large metal spoon, fold the sugar and almond mixture into the egg whites.

6. The mixture should be thoroughly incorporated and smooth – this can take up to 1 minute. When it is ready, the mixture should drop from the spoon in a smooth molten mass.

7. Fill the piping bag with the mixture and pipe evenly sized rounds to fill the circles drawn on the baking parchment on the prepared baking sheets. (If a main recipe you are following elsewhere in this book uses this Basic Macarons method, you will most likely need to resume the main recipe after this step.)

8. Tap the bottom of the baking sheets sharply, once, on the work surface to expel any large air bubbles.

9. You can scatter edible decorations, liquid food colouring etc. onto the unbaked macaron shells at this stage.

10. Leave for at least 15 minutes, and up to 1 hour, until the macarons have 'set' and formed a dry shell. They should not be sticky, tacky or wet when tested with your fingertip.

11. Meanwhile, preheat the oven to 170°C (325°F) Gas 3. Bake the macarons on the middle shelf of the preheated oven, one sheet at a time, for 12 minutes. The tops should be crisp and the bottoms dry. Leave to cool on the baking sheet.

TIPS FOR SUCCESS:
* Get your equipment ready before you start. Weigh all your ingredients carefully and bring them to room temperature.

* No two ovens are the same, so get to know your oven and do adjust your oven temperature by a few degrees if you feel it's necessary, or turn the baking sheets around halfway through baking if your oven cooks hotter in places.

* If your macarons aren't perfect the first time, don't give up – remember practice makes perfect!

Classic flavour variations

Here are four ways in which the Basic Macaron meringue on pages 6–7 can be adapted to give you simple classic flavours to enjoy time and time again.

Lemon

200 g/1½ cups icing/confectioners' sugar
100 g/⅔ cup ground almonds
120–125 g/½ cup egg whites (about 3 eggs)
a pinch of salt
40 g/3 tablespoons caster/superfine sugar
1 unwaxed lemon
yellow food colouring

Follow the Basic Macarons recipe on pages 6 and 7. Wash and dry the unwaxed lemon and finely grate the zest. Add to the macaron mixture in Step 4 with some yellow food colouring, then continue with the recipe. Fill the shells with lemon curd.

Pistachio

50 g/½ cup shelled unsalted pistachios
200 g/1½ cups icing/confectioners' sugar
75 g/½ cup ground almonds
120–125 g/½ cup egg whites (about 3 eggs)
a pinch of salt
40 g/3 tablespoons caster/superfine sugar
green food colouring

Use good-quality, unsalted shelled pistachios and grind them finely in a food processor along with the icing/confectioners' sugar and ground almonds in Step 1 of the Basic Macarons recipe on pages 6 and 7. Add the green food colouring in Step 4, then continue with the recipe. Fill the shells with Buttercream (see page 27), if liked.

Raspberry

200 g/1½ cups icing/confectioners' sugar
100 g/⅔ cup ground almonds
120–125 g/½ cup egg whites (about 3 eggs)
a pinch of salt
40 g/3 tablespoons caster/superfine sugar
raspberry flavouring
pink food colouring

Follow the Basic Macarons recipe on pages 6 and 7. Add a little raspberry flavouring and pink food colouring in Step 4, then continue with the recipe. Fill the shells with Buttercream (see page 27) or use the very best raspberry preserve, as preferred.

Chocolate

2 tablespoons good-quality cocoa powder
200 g/1½ cups minus 1 tablespoon icing/ confectioners' sugar
100 g/⅔ cup ground almonds
120–125 g/½ cup egg whites (about 3 eggs)
a pinch of salt
40 g/3 tablespoons caster/superfine sugar
red food colouring

Put the good-quality cocoa powder in a food processor along with the icing/confectioners' sugar and ground almonds in Step 1 of the Basic Macarons recipe on pages 6 and 7. Add a little red food colouring in Step 4 to boost the colour slightly, then continue with the recipe. Fill the shells with Dark Chocolate Ganache (see page 30), if liked.

Patissier's macarons

This recipe is favoured by professional pastry chefs and should be used for the novelty macarons on pages 76–139. It is best to keep this mixture unflavoured so that they delicate shells are robust enough to pipe into shapes, decorate with embellishments and assemble into designs. However, if you do want to add a flavour to your shells, use a tiny amount of strongly flavoured essence oils, which will not affect the batter too much. This batch of mixture may seem quite large for making at home but it is difficult to make it in small batches. The good news is that leftover macaron shells last for 3–5 days in the fridge but, helpfully, they also freeze very well.

145 g/5 oz. egg whites
95 g/½ cup caster/superfine sugar
170 g/1⅔ cups ground almonds
260 g/2 cups minus 2 tablespoons icing/
   confectioners' sugar

a stand mixer with whisk attachment
a rubber spatula
2 solid heavy baking sheets
a transparent silicone baking mat
non-stick baking parchment
your chosen template (see page 140)
piping bags, with a selection of tips

MAKES ABOUT 40–45 (STANDARD SIZE 5-CM/2-INCH) SHELLS BUT THIS YIELD WILL VARY ACCORDING TO THE SHAPE OF YOUR DESIGN

1. Whisk the egg whites in a stand mixer with a whisk attachment until doubled in size.

2. Add the caster/superfine sugar and continue to whisk until the meringue mixture looks glossy and starts to come away from the side of the bowl, forming one large blob in the middle. At this stage, if you lift the whisk, the meringue should form a stiff peak, holding after the whisk has been lifted. Note: When you are first learning how to make macarons, it is best to with a very stiff meringue. This means the end result can be slightly dry, but it gives you extra time at the folding stage, allowing you to get your folding technique right. If your meringue is under-whisked (or if it is perfectly whisked but you have not yet got your folding technique right), it will collapse before you have incorporated all the dry ingredients.

3. Sift the ground almonds together with the icing/confectioners' sugar in a separate bowl.

4. Add the meringue mixture to the dry ingredients.

5. Fold the meringue into the dry ingredients using quick circular movements until the mixture is ready for piping. This technique requires you

to be gentle but not too gentle – you aren't coating the meringue in the dry mixture, you need to combine the two together. As well as being gentle, you also need to work quickly, otherwise the macaron mixture will collapse. Use a spatula to fold the almonds into the meringue until there are no more almonds around the edge of the bowl. At this stage, use your spatula to scoop up the dry ingredients from the bottom of the bowl and work them into the meringue. Fold until there are no dry ingredients visible in the bowl. The mixture should not be runny.

6. Transfer the macaron mixture to a piping bag fitted with the appropriate tip as directed by the recipe you are following. To transfer the macaron mixture to your piping back without making a mess is to put the piping bag, tip-side down, into a jug/pitcher and scoop the mixture into it. Pipe your macarons as required by the recipe – see pages 12–17 for detailed instructions on piping techniques.

7. Meanwhile, preheat the oven to 160°C (325°F) Gas 3. Bake the macarons, one sheet at a time, in the preheated oven for 8 minutes, or for the length of time it advises in the individual recipe. The tops of the macarons should be crisp and the undersides should be dry.

8. Allow the macarons to cool for 30 minutes on the baking sheets. This allows the sugar to crystallize and stops the macarons from getting stuck. After 30 minutes, remove the macarons using a palette knife/metal spatula.

TIPS FOR SUCCESS:
* Separate the egg whites from the yolks 3–5 days before you plan to use them, and store them, covered in the fridge. Bring them to room temperature before baking.

* If the macarons have stuck to the sheet, it means that the meringue collapsed slightly and wasn't able to support the ground almonds. Try working with a stiffer meringue, until your folding technique has improved (see Note, step 2).

Piping macarons

USING THE TEMPLATES

There are templates provided at the back of the book on pages 140–141, including classic rounds in a choice of sizes as well as novelty shapes for the more complex recipes in the Decorated Macarons of this book (pages 76–139). To make a template, simply trace your chosen template onto a piece of baking parchment the size of your baking sheet and repeat for as many as you can fit, leaving a gap between them. Place the template you have made on a solid heavy baking sheet and place a transparent silicone mat on top, so that you can see the template through the mat. (Alternatively, you can just pipe directly onto the sheet of baking parchment, but this isn't advised if you are using a fan oven, as the sheets can end up blowing around the oven and spoiling the macarons.) You should be able to fit about 12 standard shells (5-cm/2-inch rounds) on an average baking sheet, so use two baking sheets to make a batch of 12 filled macarons.

PIPING TECHNIQUES

Grip the top of the bag with the thumb and index finger of your writing hand, then, using the rest of your fingers, wrap your hand round the top of the bag. Pick the bag up and turn it over. Imagine the piping bag is an apple and you are holding the stalk between your thumb and index finger and using the rest of your fingers to grab the apple.

Squeeze the mixture gently, until it is tight in the piping bag and there is no air trapped inside. Use your other hand to pull the top of the bag gently, if needed, to tighten the bag. Now you are ready to pipe. You only pipe with your writing hand; your other hand should just guide the tip, but not squeeze. You can only control the amount you pipe by using one hand.

Position the tip right in the middle of the circle and pipe in the same place, until the macaron mixture pushes out to the edge of the template. Stop piping and quickly flick the tip up and away.

At this stage, if you touch the macaron with your finger, it will be very sticky. Therefore, you need to let the macarons rest for 15–30 minutes before you cook them. After this time, a layer of skin will have formed over the top of the macarons. When the macarons go in the oven, the hot air pushes against the crust and creates the typical macaron shape with the classic 'foot' at the bottom.

Piping face shapes

For most animal shapes, use a standard 5-cm/ 2-inch round template. Trace the template from page 140 onto some baking parchment to create about 12 circles, or as many as you can fit on your baking sheet. Place the template onto a flat, heavy baking sheet and place a transparent silicone mat on top so that you can see the template through it.

Pointy ears: For pointy ears such as cats' ears (see recipe, page 95), follow the instructions on page 12 for piping rounds. Once you have piped a round, use a sugar-working tool or toothpick to drag the macaron mixture away from the circle into a pointy ear (see pictures, opposite). Repeat for the second ear.

Round ears: For round ears, such as bears' ears (see recipe, page 92), follow the instructions on page 12 for piping rounds. Once you have piped a round, use a smaller tip to pipe a blob of macaron mixture for each ear that is just touching the edge of the main circle.

Long ears: For long ears, such as bunnies' ears (see recipe, page 103), follow the instructions on page 12 for piping rounds. Once you have piped a round, use a small tip and start piping at the top of the ear, working towards the piped macaron circle. When you reach the piped circle, stop piping and quickly flick the tip up and away from the macaron surface.

Piping heart shapes

Heart-shaped macarons make a charming gift for a loved one (see the Be My Valentine recipe, page 78).

To pipe hearts, you will need to use a slightly smaller tip than you would use if you were piping rounds – 8-mm/⅜-inch is a good size for this task.

Trace the Heart template from page 140 onto some baking parchment to create about 12 hearts, or as many as you can fit on your baking sheet.

Place the baking parchment with the drawn template onto a flat, heavy baking sheet and place a transparent silicone mat on top so that you can see the Heart template through the mat.

Position the tip at the top left of the heart, pipe down to the bottom then up to the top left of the heart, and move the tip back down again to make sure that the template is filled. Stop piping and quickly flick the tip up and away from the macaron surface.

Piping joined macarons

For joined macarons (see the Crawling Caterpillar recipe, page 99 and Tetris page 109), trace the relvant template for the macaron you are making from (see pages 140–141) onto some baking parchment. Create as many as you can fit on your baking sheet.

Place the baking parchment with the drawn template onto a flat, heavy baking sheet and place a transparent silicone mat on top so that you can see the joined template through it.

Pipe each macaron individually (as shown below). Position the tip right in the middle of the circle and pipe in the same place, until the macaron mixture pushes out to the edge of the circle. Stop piping and quickly flick the tip up and away from the macaron surface. Note that the macarons should not join together while you are piping them – this will occur when the macaron mixture expands during resting and before baking.

Handle your joined macarons carefully once they are baked and you are adding fillings, to avoid snapping them. But if you do, your filling may help hold them in place so don't despair.

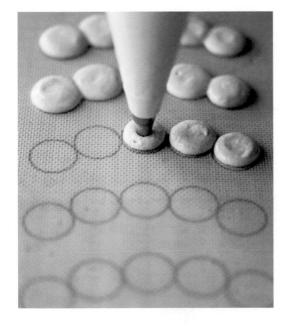

Decorating Techniques

Hand painting macarons

There are so many ways to transform a simple macaron into a work of art. You can create stunning effects on the surface of a baked and cooled macaron by hand with a range of paintbrushes and edible paints.

To create edible paints, you just need to dilute a small amount of food colouring (about ½ teaspoon) in a few drops of food colouring rejuvenator spirit/thinner. This can be bought online or in specialist cake decorating stores. Add enough to create a liquid paint, mixing well.

Use a clean flat paintbrush for large brush strokes (see the Father's Day Black & Gold recipe, page 86) and a fine paintbrush for thin lines (see the Cherry Blossom recipe, on page 127 and the step-by-step technique shown opposite). You can paint flowers, flags, letters of the alphabet or abstract designs or whatever you choose. Try different shapes and sizes of paintbrush for different effects; just remember to make sure it is very clean and hasn't been used previously for non-edible paints.

Working with royal icing

Royal Icing can be used to decorate macarons with line art, it can be used to create run-outs, and it is also very useful as the edible 'glue' for sticking embellishments onto macaron shells (see facing page) or for assembling shells in stacks (see page 25). It's quite difficult to make a small batch of icing, as a small amount of egg white is tricky to whisk. Therefore, it is better to make the batch even if it means you may waste some. It's better than trying to make a small batch and wasting it all!

90 g/3⅙ oz. egg whites
480 g/3⅓ cups icing/confectioners' sugar
2 tablespoons freshly squeezed lemon juice

MAKES ABOUT 600 G/21 OZ.

Place the egg whites, two-thirds of the sugar and the lemon juice into the bowl of a stand mixer fitted with the paddle attachment, and beat for about 10 minutes, until white and thick. Alternatively, use a mixing bowl and hand-held electric whisk. Add the remaining sugar and beat until stiff. If you are not using it immediately, cover the icing with a damp kitchen towel and leave at room temperature to prevent it from drying out.

Colouring royal icing: Add food colouring using a toothpick and stir until the icing is an even shade. Add the food colouring a little at a time, as you can always add more! If you need multiple colours, split the batch of icing into portions in separate bowls and colour each one individually.

Piping Royal Icing: You can make a simple piping bag for icing from a sheet of baking parchment. Simply roll the parchment into a cone and secure with a small piece of sticky tape. It is a good idea to practise piping onto a sheet of baking parchment before you start piping onto your macaron shells.

Adding embellishments

There is a huge variety of sugar decorations available to buy today – you can buy them in specialist baking stores, as well as from online retailers. In the Decorated Macarons section of this book (see pages 76–139), different sugar decorations are used to create very pretty effects. With a steady hand, it is easier than it looks to achieve shimmering, edible details on your macarons.

When adding sugar diamonds and pearls (see the Jewelled Birthday Crown, page 84 and Precious Gems, page 90), you will need to prepare a batch of Royal Icing (see recipe on opposite page). Put the icing in a small piping bag and snip off the end to create a small hole. Pipe a dot of Royal Icing onto the centre of the macaron shell. Use it to stick a sugar diamond to the shell. Stick sugar pearls around the diamonds using more dots of Royal Icing.

Use tweezers if necessary when applying very small decorations. A pair of tweezers is useful for placing decorations onto macaron shells, so it's a good idea to buy a pair that you keep just for baking purposes. Allow any decoration you have applied to dry for 1 hour before serving or packaging your macarons.

Lace techniques

This is a simple technique that is used for the Something Blue recipe, page 89, and it creates very impressive results. Packs of cake lace can be bought from online retailers, and they come with specific instructions on how to use each particular brand. However, the basic technique remains largely the same and is as follows:

Place the recommended amount of water in the bowl of a stand mixer fitted with a whisk attachment (or use a mixing bowl and hand-held electric whisk) and add the amount of powder specified on the packet instructions.

Mix on medium-high speed for 2 minutes, or as recommended, then add the amount of liquid specified on the packet instructions. Mix on medium-high speed for 5–8 minutes, or until the mixture is smooth. Pour the mixture onto the lace silicone mat and spread it out using a knife. Make sure there is cake lace mixture in all the moulds, then use the knife to remove the excess mixture. Allow to dry at room temperature for 6–8 hours or place in a very low oven for 10–15 minutes.

To release the lace, place the mould face-down on a sheet of baking parchment and peel the mould away, using a knife to help you release the cake lace.

To adhere the lace to your baked and cooled macaron shells, moisten the macaron shell with a little water, then press the lace on to it and allow to dry.

Making sugarpaste decorations

Sugarpaste is also known as ready-to-roll icing. It can be bought in various colours, but for this book it is best to buy white and add your own colouring, unless you need a good selection of colours (see the Merry & Bright Baubles recipe, page 139). It is mostly because you will often need only a very small amount of sugarpaste, so you can just cut off the amount you need and seal the rest up tightly for another time. It does also give you much more control over the colour you use, and you can make your colour darker, more vibrant or paler to suit your needs.

To colour sugarpaste, use a toothpick to add a small amount of food colouring paste (or use the amount specified in the recipe, if it specifies an exact amount). Place the sugarpaste on a clean work surface lightly dusted with icing/confectioners' sugar, and knead it until it is an even shade. Remember, use a little bit of food colouring paste first – you can always add more if needed, but you cannot take it away!

To create shapes, dust the surface of the sugarpaste well with icing/confectioners' sugar and lay a sheet of baking parchment over the top. Use a rolling pin to roll the sugarpaste out to the desired thickness. Next use mini cutters to cut out shapes such as hearts or flowers and set them aside to dry before using them to decorate your macarons.

You can use Royal Icing (see page 20) as a glue to stick you decorations to baked and cooled macarons.

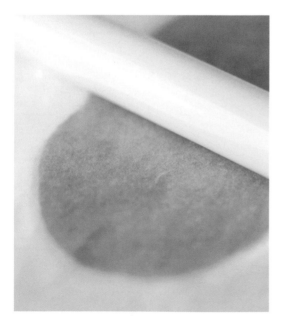

Assembling macarons

There is much more to macarons than a pair of macaron shells, sandwiched together around a filling. You can stack shells to create different shapes and create characters, such as animal bodies, as shown in the Sleepy Cats recipe (see page 95), Three Little Piggies (see page 96) and Pudgy Pandas (see page 104).

You can also create multi-layered faces to give depth and character to your animals, such as the Teddy Bears recipe on page 92, where the nose is made from a smaller macaron shell baked in a contrasting shade of brown which also helps to add depth to the design.

You will need a batch of Royal Icing (see page 20). It's best to decorate the face first, then allow the Royal Icing to dry so that you don't smudge it when you stick it to the filled macaron body. Make the body with 2 shells of the same colour, sandwich them together with a filling and chill for 12 hours before you attach the final decorated macaron to finish the design. Use Royal Icing to stick the head onto the body, then allow to dry before serving.

Alternatively, you can also stick the head onto the side on the body (again, see Sleepy Cats, page 95), or make the heads with a smaller template (see Three Little Piggies, page 96). Experiment with different animals and you will come up with your own ideas for assembling macarons and create your own unique designs.

Filling Macarons

Filling your macarons is the fun bit! There is such a vast range of fillings you can use (see recipes pages 27–31), but easy and instant fillings to try include the following:

- jam/jelly or fruit preserves
- chocolate spread
- chocolate-hazelnut spread (such as Nutella)
- toffee spread (dulce de leche)
- marshmallow fluff
- sharp fruit curds, such as lemon or blackcurrant
- nut butters, such as peanut and almond butter
- whipped cream
- sweetened mascarpone
- crème fraîche

To fill macarons, match up your shells into pairs of the same colour, shape and/or size. Line them up in rows of pairs, placing one shell from each pair flat-side up and the other flat-side down.

For a professional finish, pipe circles of filling using a piping bag fitted with a small round tip. Alternatively, use a palette knife or metal spatula to spread the filling onto the shells. You will need about 1 teaspoonful of filling for standard shells.

Pipe or spread the filling onto the flat-side of one macaron shell in each pair, then top with the flat-side of the other shell, pressing them together gently. Allow to set in the fridge for 12 hours, unless the filling contains fresh fruit, in which case it should be chilled for only 1–2 hours.

Buttercream

This light and fluffy filling is used for many of the novelty macarons in this book as it can be flavoured with everything from jams/jellies, chopped fresh or dried fruit to rose cordial and peppermint essence.

300 g/1½ cups caster/superfine sugar
5 large/US extra large egg whites
500 g/4½ sticks unsalted butter, cut into pieces
2 teaspoons vanilla powder or seeds of 1 vanilla pod/bean

MAKES 800 G/28 OZ.

Place the sugar and egg whites into the bowl of a stand mixer or a heatproof mixing bowl and set over a pan of gently simmering water. Whisk using a hand-held electric whisk for 3 minutes, until the sugar has dissolved and the egg whites are hot to the touch. Transfer the bowl to the stand mixer fitted with the whisk attachment, if using.

Whisk on high speed in the mixer or with a hand-held electric whisk, until the mixture has cooled down and formed stiff peaks; about 8 minutes.

Switch to the paddle attachment. Add the butter, one piece at a time, and beat until incorporated. Don't worry if the mixture appears curdled after all the butter has been added; it will become smooth again with beating. Beat until smooth.

If using within several hours, cover with clingfilm/plastic wrap and keep in a cool room. Alternatively, store in the fridge for 3 days. Beat to soften before use.

Vanilla Cream

Nothing beats the flavour of real vanilla. This deliciously creamy filling can be used to fill most of the macarons in the book, but works particularly well with the addition of some finely chopped strawberries or raspberries.

3 egg yolks
75 g/¾ cup caster/superfine sugar
1 tablespoon cornflour/cornstarch
250 ml/1 cup full-fat milk
1 vanilla pod/bean, split lengthways
3 tablespoons unsalted butter, diced
100 ml/½ cup double/heavy cream

MAKES ABOUT 400 G/2 CUPS

Put the egg yolks, sugar and cornflour/cornstarch in a small, heatproof bowl and whisk together until combined.

Heat the milk, along with the vanilla pod/bean, in a small saucepan until it only just starts to boil. Remove the vanilla and pour the hot milk over the egg mixture, whisking constantly until smooth.

Pour the mixture back into the pan and cook gently over low heat, stirring constantly until the custard comes to the boil and thickens.

Strain into a clean bowl, add the butter and stir until the butter has melted and is incorporated into the mixture. Cover the surface with clingfilm/plastic wrap and leave to cool before refrigerating.

Whip the cream until it will hold soft peaks and fold into the chilled custard. Keep chilled until ready to use.

Caramel Chocolate Ganache

This delicious ganache is made with 'blonde' chocolate which is actually caramelized white chocolate. It has a light beige hue and tastes creamy and toasty. It's good with chocolate- or coffee-flavoured macaron shells.

150 g/scant 1 cup good-quality blonde chocolate (ideally Valrhona), broken into pieces
300 ml/1¼ cups whipping cream
180 g/1 cup minus 1½ tablespoons caster/granulated sugar
1 teaspoon vanilla powder
50 g/3½ tablespoons unsalted butter
1½ teaspoons salt

MAKES 650 G/23 OZ.

Place the cream in a saucepan and heat over medium heat until just about to boil. Place the sugar in a saucepan and heat, without stirring, until the sugar has melted and you have a golden caramel. Swirl the pan occasionally, if needed.

Add the hot cream and stir to mix. Use a sugar thermometer to measure the temperature, then heat over medium heat until the mixture reaches 104°C/219°F. As soon as it reaches this temperature, remove the caramel from the heat and immerse the bottom of the pan briefly in a sink of cold water to stop the cooking.

Let the temperature drop to 75°C/167°F, then add, a little at a time, to the chocolate. Stir well after each addition to make sure the chocolate is fully melted. When the mixture reaches 35°C/95°F, add the softened butter and blend. Allow to cool to room temperature, then leave in a cold place for 24 hours. Ganache doesn't react well to being stored in the fridge, so find a cold room of your house. However, in the summer, or if your house is warm, you will need to use the fridge. After this time, the ganache should be a nice spreadable consistency.

TIPS FOR SUCCESS:
Make sure you choose the right cream for your ganache. Whipping cream has a fat content somewhere between single/light and double/heavy cream, which makes it ideal for making ganache. Double/heavy cream is very oily and can split, and single/light cream doesn't contain enough fat.

Dark chocolate ganache

A classic velvety smooth ganache made with dark/bittersweet chocolate and whipping cream. Simple but so rich and delicious that the basic mixture is what chocolatiers use to make hand-rolled chocolate truffles. Use it to fill macarons and when you want to add a dark, sophisticated touch.

200 g/1⅓ cups good-quality dark/ bittersweet chocolate, broken into pieces (use chocolate with 70% cocoa solids)
120 ml/8 tablespoons whipping cream (see Tip on page 29)
50 g/3½ tablespoons unsalted butter

MAKES 500 G/18 OZ.

Melt the chocolate in a microwave or in a heatproof bowl set over a pan of barely simmering water, stirring regularly.

Place the cream in a saucepan and heat over medium heat until it is just about to boil. Pour about one-third of the cream over the chocolate and stir with a rubber spatula gently, until blended. Add a little more cream and stir again until smooth. Keep adding the cream gradually, until you have added it all and the mixture is silky and smooth.

Allow the ganache to cool to 30°C/86°F, the stir in the butter, a little at a time.

If you add the butter when the ganache is too hot, it will split.

Cover the ganache with clingfilm/plastic wrap, pressing it onto the surface of the ganache to stop a skin from forming. Allow to cool to room temperature, then leave in a cold place for 24 hours. Ganache doesn't react well to being stored in the fridge, so find a cold room of your house. However, in the summer, or if your house is warm, you will need to use the fridge. After this time, the ganache should be a nice spreadable consistency.

White chocolate ganache

Choosing white chocolate for ganache is very difficult to get right when following a recipe, as the consistency of white chocolate varies so much from manufacturer to manufacturer. This recipe works well using either Valrhona Opalys or Vahrhona Ivoire which you can buy online (see Suppliers, page 144). If you use a different brand of white chocolate, the results may vary a little, but always choose a good quality one.

230 g/1½ cups good-quality white
   chocolate, broken into pieces
120 ml/8 tablespoons whipping
   cream (see Tip on page 29)
50 g/3½ tablespoons unsalted
   butter

MAKES 500 G/18 OZ.

Melt the chocolate in a microwave or in a heatproof bowl set over a pan of barely simmering water, stirring regularly.

Place the cream in a saucepan and heat over medium heat until it is just about to boil. Pour about one-third of the cream over the chocolate and stir with a rubber spatula gently, until blended. Add a little more cream and stir again until smooth. Keep adding the cream gradually, until you have added it all and the mixture is silky and smooth.

Allow the ganache to cool to 30°C/86°F, the stir in the butter, a little at a time. If you add the butter when the ganache is too hot, it will split.

Cover the ganache with clingfilm/plastic wrap, pressing it onto the surface of the ganache to stop a skin from forming. Allow to cool to room temperature, then leave in a cold place for 24 hours. Ganache doesn't react well to being stored in the fridge, so find a cold room of your house. However, in the summer, or if your house is warm, you will need to use the fridge. After this time, the ganache should be a nice spreadable consistency.

Classic macarons

Once you've mastered the art and technique of simple macarons, you can let your imagination run wild with flavours and colours. Natural oils and extracts are a great way of flavouring your macaron shells, from violet to toffee apple. The flavoured macaron recipes in this section take the traditional flavours as their starting point, and then add fillings to bring them to life.

Fruit & flowers

White chocolate & raspberry

Lightly dip the bristles of a clean toothbrush into liquid food colouring. Using your fingertips, 'flick' the bristles over uncooked macarons for a Jackson Pollock effect.

1 quantity Basic Macarons recipe (see page 6)
1 teaspoon vanilla extract
red liquid food colouring

FILLING
½ quantity White Chocolate Ganache (see page 31)
200 g/1½ cups fresh raspberries

2 solid baking sheets lined with baking parchment
a clean toothbrush
a piping bag, fitted with a star-shaped tip

MAKES 20

Prepare the Basic Macarons mixture according to the recipe on page 6, adding the vanilla extract to the meringue mixture in Step 4.

Pipe rounds of mixture onto the prepared baking sheets. Tap the baking sheets sharply on the work surface. Trickle a little red food colouring onto a saucer, then dip the clean toothbrush into it. Flick the bristles over the macarons so that they are flecked with red. Leave the macarons to rest for 15 minutes–1 hour.

Preheat the oven to 170°C (325°F) Gas 3.

Bake the macarons in the preheated oven, one sheet at a time, for 10 minutes. Leave to cool on the baking sheet.

Fill the piping bag with the White Chocolate Ganache and pipe 4 rosettes near the edge of half the macaron shells. Place a raspberry between each rosette and sandwich with the remaining macaron shells. Leave to rest for 30 minutes before serving.

Blueberry & vanilla

Try piping these macarons into delicate fingers instead of the usual round shapes and fill with blueberry purée, fresh blueberries and a delicate vanilla cream.

1 quantity Basic Macarons recipe (see page 6)
purple food colouring
pink or purple sugar sprinkles

FILLING
300 g/3 cups fresh blueberries
1 tablespoon granulated sugar
1 quantity Vanilla Cream (see page 28)

2 solid baking sheets lined with baking parchment
a piping bag, fitted with a star-shaped tip

MAKES 20

Prepare the Basic Macarons mixture according to the recipe on page 6, adding purple food colouring to the meringue mixture in Step 4.

Pipe 6-cm/2½-inch-long fingers (instead of rounds) of mixture onto the prepared baking sheets. Tap the baking sheets sharply on the work surface, then scatter sugar sprinkles over the tops. Leave the macarons to rest for 15 minutes–1 hour.

Preheat the oven to 170°C (325°F) Gas 3.

Bake the macarons in the preheated oven, one sheet at a time, for 10 minutes. Leave to cool on the baking sheet.

To make the filling, tip half the blueberries into a small saucepan, add the sugar and 1 tablespoon water and cook over medium heat until the berries soften and burst, then continue to cook until reduced and thickened to a jam-/jelly-like consistency. Transfer to a nylon sieve/strainer, press through into a small bowl and set aside to cool.

Spread the filling over half the macaron shells and arrange the whole blueberries on top, spaced apart. Pipe the vanilla cream between the blueberries and top with the remaining macaron shells.

Apple & blackberry

Here's a classic autumnal fruit combination that works perfectly in macarons not only because it tastes great, but also because the colours complement each other.

1 quantity Basic Macarons
recipe (see page 6)
purple food colouring
green food colouring

FILLING
4 small dessert apples,
e.g. Cox's or Winesap
1 tablespoon granulated
sugar
freshly squeezed juice of
½ lemon
125 g/1 cup blackberries
100 ml/½ cup double/
heavy cream

2 solid baking sheets, lined
with baking parchment
a piping bag, fitted with a
star-shaped tip

MAKES 20

Prepare the filling before you make the macaron shells.

Peel, core and roughly chop the apples and place in a medium saucepan with the sugar and lemon juice. Cover and cook over low heat until the fruit has started to soften, stirring from time to time. Add the blackberries and continue to cook for a further 10–15 minutes until the fruit has reduced to a thick purée. Remove from the heat and press through a nylon sieve/strainer into a small bowl. Taste and add a little more sugar, if needed.

Prepare the Basic Macarons mixture according to the recipe on page 6, but when you get to Step 4, divide the mixture between two bowls and add purple food colouring to one bowl and green food colouring to the other.

Pipe 20 rounds of each colour of mixture onto each prepared baking sheet. Tap the baking sheets sharply on the work surface and leave the macarons to rest for 15 minutes–1 hour.

Preheat the oven to 170°C (325°F) Gas 3.

Bake the macarons in the preheated oven, one sheet at a time, for 10 minutes. Leave to cool on the baking sheet.

Lightly whip the cream. Spread the fruit filling onto the purple macaron shells. Fill the piping bag with the whipped cream and pipe it onto the green shells. Sandwich the two together and leave to rest for about 30 minutes before serving.

Raspberry & passion fruit

I love fruit curds and this raspberry and passion fruit one used as
a filling is no exception. You may need to add food colouring to it
to make it a punchier pink.

1 quantity Basic Macarons
 recipe (see page 6)
red or pink food
 colouring

FILLING
125 g/1 cup fresh
 raspberries
2 passion fruit
3 egg yolks
50 g/¼ cup caster/
 superfine sugar
50 g/3 tablespoons
 unsalted butter, diced

2 solid baking sheets, lined
 with baking parchment

MAKES 20

Prepare the Basic Macarons mixture according to the recipe on page 6,
adding red or pink food colouring to the meringue mixture in Step 4.

Pipe rounds of mixture onto the prepared baking sheets. Tap the
baking sheets sharply on the work surface and leave the macarons to
rest for 15 minutes–1 hour.

Preheat the oven to 170°C (325°F) Gas 3.

Bake the macarons in the preheated oven, one sheet at a time, for
10 minutes. Leave to cool on the baking sheet.

To make the filling, whizz the raspberries in a food processor, then
press through a nylon sieve/strainer into a medium heatproof bowl.
Cut the passion fruit in half, scoop the seeds and juice into the
raspberry bowl and add the egg yolks, sugar and unsalted butter.
Set the bowl over a pan of simmering water and cook for about 10–15
minutes, stirring from time to time until the curd has thickened and
will coat the back of a spoon. Strain into a clean bowl and add a tiny
amount of red or pink food colouring if you need to accentuate the
raspberry colour. Cover the surface of the curd with clingfilm/plastic
wrap and leave to cool before refrigerating for a couple of hours.

Spread the filling over half the macaron shells and sandwich with
the other half. Leave to rest for about 30 minutes before serving.

Coconut & mango

The taste of the tropics! If you can find them, use super-sweet, flavoursome Alphonso mangoes.

1 quantity Basic Macarons
   recipe (see page 6)
2 tablespoons desiccated/
   dried shedded coconut
yellow food colouring

FILLING
1 ripe mango
1 tablespoon palm sugar
   or light brown sugar
1 tablespoon dark rum
100 g/3½ oz. white
   chocolate, finely
   chopped
freshly squeezed lime
   juice, to taste

2 solid baking sheets, lined
   with baking parchment

MAKES 20

Prepare the Basic Macarons mixture according to the recipe on page 6, adding the desiccated/dried shedded coconut to the food processor in Step 1. Then add yellow food colouring to the meringue mixture in Step 4.

Pipe rounds of mixture onto the prepared baking sheets. Tap the baking sheets sharply on the work surface and leave the macarons to rest for 15 minutes–1 hour.

Preheat the oven to 170°C (325°F) Gas 3.

Bake the macarons in the preheated oven, one sheet at a time, for 10 minutes. Leave to cool on the baking sheet.

To make the filling, slice the cheeks off the mango, score the flesh into dice and cut away from the skin. Tip the flesh into a small saucepan with the sugar and rum. Cook over low–medium heat until the mango is very soft and starting to caramelize. Remove from the heat and leave to cool slightly, then add the white chocolate and whizz in the food processor until smooth. Add squeezed lime juice to taste – you will probably only need 1 teaspoonful to balance the flavours.

Scoop the mango filling into a bowl and leave to cool before covering and refrigerating until ready to use.

Spread the filling over half the macaron shells and sandwich with the other half. Leave to rest for about 30 minutes before serving.

Rose

You could make boxes of these dainty rose-infused macarons in varying shades of pink – perfect for an afternoon tea with the girls.

1 quantity Basic Macarons recipe (see page 6)
pink food colouring
½ teaspoon rose water
1 tablespoon rose sprinkles or crystallized rose petals, finely chopped

FILLING
½ quantity Buttercream (see page 27, using ½ teaspoon rose water)

2 solid baking sheets, lined with baking parchment
a piping bag, fitted with a star-shaped tip

MAKES 20

Prepare the Basic Macarons mixture according to the recipe on page 6, adding pink food colouring and the rose water to the meringue mixture in Step 4.

Pipe rounds of mixture onto the prepared baking sheets. Tap the baking sheets sharply on the work surface, then scatter rose sprinkles or petals over the tops. Leave the macarons to rest for 15 minutes–1 hour.

Preheat the oven to 170°C (325°F) Gas 3.

Bake the macarons in the preheated oven, one sheet at a time, for 10 minutes. Leave to cool on the baking sheet.

Fill the piping bag with the rose-flavoured buttercream and pipe it onto half the macaron shells. Sandwich with the other half and leave to rest for about 30 minutes before serving.

Violet creams

Reminiscent of boxes of violet fondant cream chocolates, all the elements are here but in a macaron. Consult the stockists on page 144 for violet flavouring.

1 quantity Basic Macarons recipe (see page 6)
1–2 teaspoons violet flavouring (see page 144)
purple food colouring

FILLING
½ quantity Dark Chocolate Ganache (see page 30)
½ quantity White Chocolate Ganache (see page 31)

2 solid baking sheets, lined with baking parchment
2 piping bags, fitted with star-shaped tips

MAKES ABOUT 30

Prepare the Basic Macarons mixture according to the recipe on page 6, adding the violet flavouring and some purple food colouring to the meringue mixture in Step 4.

Pipe 2.5-cm/1-inch rounds of mixture onto the prepared baking sheets. Tap the baking sheets sharply on the work surface and leave the macarons to rest for 15 minutes–1 hour.

Preheat the oven to 170°C (325°F) Gas 3.

Bake the macarons in the preheated oven, one sheet at a time, for 7 minutes. Leave to cool on the baking sheet.

Fill each piping bag with the prepared ganaches. Pipe one ganache over one-quarter of the macaron shells and sandwich together with another quarter. Repeat with the other ganache and the remaining macaron shells. Leave to rest for about 30 minutes before serving.

Chocolate & coffee

Chocolate & cherry

Black Forest gâteau in a macaron. Dried cherries are an excellent baking ingredients – soaked in sweet booze, here they are a sublime partner for rich chocolate.

1 quantity Chocolate
  Macarons recipe
  (see page 9)

FILLING
75 g/½ cup dried sour
  cherries
1–2 tablespoons cherry
  brandy
1 tablespoon granulated
  sugar
½ quantity Dark
  Chocolate Ganache
  (see page 30)
100 ml/½ cup double/
  heavy cream

*2 solid baking sheets, lined
  with baking parchment*

MAKES 20

Prepare the filling before you make the macaron shells.

Put the dried cherries in a small saucepan with the brandy, sugar and 2 tablespoons water. Set over low heat and bring to just below boiling point. Remove from the heat and leave the cherries to soak for at least 2 hours. They will absorb the liquid and become plump and juicy.

Meanwhile, put the Dark Chocolate Ganache in the fridge to thicken. Prepare the Chocolate Macarons according to the recipe on page 9.

Pipe rounds of mixture onto the prepared baking sheets. Tap the baking sheets sharply on the work surface and leave the macarons to rest for 15 minutes–1 hour.

Preheat the oven to 170°C (325°F) Gas 3.

Bake the macarons in the preheated oven, one sheet at a time, for 10 minutes. Leave to cool on the baking sheet.

Tip the soaked cherries and any remaining juice into a food processor and blend until well chopped but not smooth. Lightly whip the cream and fold it into the chopped cherry mixture.

Spread the Dark Chocolate Ganache onto half the macaron shells. Spread cherry cream onto the remaining macaron shells and sandwich the two together. Leave to rest for 30 minutes before serving.

Blackcurrant & chocolate

This is one of those flavours that creeps up on you after the first bite: first you taste the deep chocolatey-ness and then the blackcurrant sneaks in and takes over.

1 quantity Basic Macarons recipe (see page 6)
purple food colouring

FILLING
125 g/1 generous cup fresh or frozen blackcurrants
1–2 tablespoons granulated sugar
1 tablespoon crème de cassis (blackcurrant liqueur)
100 ml/½ cup double/ heavy cream
½ tablespoon light muscovado/light brown sugar
100 g/3½ oz. dark/ bittersweet chocolate, finely chopped

2 solid baking sheets, lined with baking parchment

MAKES 20

Prepare the filling before making the macaron shells.

Tip the blackcurrants into a small saucepan, add the sugar and 1 tablespoon water and cook over low heat until the currants are very soft and juicy. Remove from the heat and press through a nylon sieve/ strainer into a bowl. Taste and add a little more sugar, if needed. Return the purée to the pan along with the crème de cassis and cook over low heat, stirring constantly, until reduced to 4 tablespoons.

Put the cream and muscovado/brown sugar in a small saucepan and bring to the boil. Tip the chocolate into a heatproof bowl, pour the hot cream over it and mix until smooth. Stir in the blackcurrant purée and leave until cool, then cover and refrigerate until ready to use.

Prepare the Basic Macarons mixture according to the recipe on page 6, adding purple food colouring to the meringue mixture in Step 4.

Pipe rounds of mixture onto the prepared baking sheets. Tap the baking sheets sharply on the work surface and leave the macarons to rest for 15 minutes–1 hour.

Preheat the oven to 170°C (325°F) Gas 3.

Bake the macarons in the preheated oven, one sheet at a time, for 10 minutes. Leave to cool on the baking sheet.

Spread the filling over half the macaron shells and sandwich with the other half. Leave to rest for about 30 minutes before serving.

Chocolate & passion fruit

First you taste the chocolate, and then the passion fruit flavour hits you in an unexpected way. These are deliciously decadent macarons so make them for a special occasion.

1 quantity Basic Macarons recipe (see page 6)
yellow food colouring
chocolate sprinkles or flakes

FILLING
6 passion fruit
½ quantity Dark Chocolate Ganache (see page 30)

2 solid baking sheets, lined with baking parchment

MAKES 20

Prepare the Basic Macarons mixture according to the recipe on page 6, adding yellow food colouring to the meringue mixture in Step 4.

Pipe rounds of mixture onto the prepared baking sheets. Tap the baking sheets sharply on the work surface, then scatter the chocolate sprinkles over the tops. Leave the macarons to rest for 15 minutes–1 hour.

Preheat the oven to 170°C (325°F) Gas 3.

Bake the macarons in the preheated oven, one sheet at a time, for 10 minutes. Leave to cool on the baking sheet.

To make the filling, cut the passion fruit in half and scoop the seeds and juice into a nylon sieve/strainer set over a small saucepan. Using the back of spoon, press the pulp through the sieve – you should end up with about 4–5 tablespoons of juice. Set the pan over low–medium heat and bring slowly to the boil. Cook gently until the juice has reduced by half and you have about 1–2 tablespoons thick passion fruit juice remaining.

Stir the thick passion fruit juice into the Dark Chocolate Ganache, then spread over half the macaron shells. Sandwich with the remaining macaron shells and leave to rest for 30 minutes before serving.

Coconut & chocolate

The addition of coconut to macaron shells makes them just a hint more delicious, if that's possible.

1 quantity Basic Macarons recipe (see page 6)
3 tablespoons desiccated/ dried shredded coconut

FILLING
150 ml/⅔ cup double/ heavy cream
½ quantity Dark Chocolate Ganache (see page 30)

2 solid baking sheets, lined with baking parchment

MAKES 20

Prepare the Basic Macarons mixture according to the recipe on page 6, adding 2 tablespoons of the desiccated/dried shredded coconut to the food processor in Step 1.

Pipe rounds of mixture onto the prepared baking sheets. Tap the baking sheets sharply on the work surface, then scatter the remaining tablespoon of desiccated/dried shredded coconut over the tops. Leave the macarons to rest for 15 minutes–1 hour.

Preheat the oven to 170°C (325°F) Gas 3.

Bake the macarons in the preheated oven, one sheet at a time, for 10 minutes. Leave to cool on the baking sheet.

To make the filling, lightly whip the cream. Spread the cream onto half the macaron shells. Spread the Dark Chocolate Ganache onto the remaining macaron shells and sandwich the two together. Leave to rest for 30 minutes before serving.

Mint & chocolate

If you thought after-dinner mints were irresistible, try these and you'll be converted. Bake a box of them and bring to a dinner party as a gift.

1 quantity Basic Macarons recipe (see page 6)
green food colouring

FILLING
25 g/1 oz. fresh mint leaves
40 g/3 tablespoons caster/superfine sugar
150 g/5 oz. dark/ bittersweet chocolate, finely chopped

2 solid baking sheets, lined with baking parchment

MAKES 20

Prepare the filling before you make the macaron shells.

Lightly crush the mint leaves between your hands and place in a small saucepan with the sugar and 100 ml/½ cup water. Slowly bring to the boil so that the sugar dissolves, then simmer gently for about 3 minutes. Remove from the heat and set aside to infuse for at least 1 hour.

Tip the chocolate into a heatproof bowl. Bring the mint syrup back to the boil, then strain into the chopped chocolate. Stir until melted and smooth. Leave to cool and thicken slightly before using.

Prepare the Basic Macarons mixture according to the recipe on page 6, adding green food colouring to the meringue mixture in Step 4.

Pipe rounds of mixture onto the prepared baking sheets. Tap the baking sheets sharply on the work surface and leave the macarons to rest for 15 minutes–1 hour.

Preheat the oven to 170°C (325°F) Gas 3.

Bake the macarons in the preheated oven, one sheet at a time, for 10 minutes. Leave to cool on the baking sheet.

Spread the filling over half the macaron shells and sandwich with the other half. Leave to rest for 30 minutes before serving.

Malted milk & chocolate

Serve these macarons with a dipping sauce of warm, deeply rich, malted hot chocolate. Swap your evening cup of cocoa for this deliciously decadent treat.

1 quantity Basic Macarons recipe (see page 6)
2 tablespoons malted milk powder
cocoa powder, for dusting

FILLING
½ quantity Dark Chocolate Ganache (see page 30)
1 tablespoon malted milk powder

2 solid baking sheets, lined with baking parchment

MAKES 20

Prepare the Basic Macarons mixture according to the recipe on page 6, adding the malted milk powder to the food processor in Step 1.

Pipe rounds of mixture onto the prepared baking sheets. Tap the baking sheets sharply on the work surface, then lightly dust cocoa powder over the tops. Leave the macarons to rest for 15 minutes–1 hour.

Preheat the oven to 170°C (325°F) Gas 3.

Bake the macarons in the preheated oven, one sheet at a time, for 10 minutes. Leave to cool on the baking sheet.

To make the filling, prepare the Dark Chocolate Ganache according to the recipe on page 30, adding the malted milk powder to the hot cream.

Spread the filling over half the macaron shells and sandwich with the other half. Leave to rest for about 30 minutes before serving.

Cappuccino

Pipe the filling into these delicate coffee-flavoured macarons in an extra-thick layer. Alternatively, you could fill the shells with Dark Chocolate Ganache (see page 30) flavoured with coffee extract to create mocha macarons.

1 quantity Basic Macarons recipe (see page 6)
2 teaspoons coffee extract or 2 teaspoons instant coffee granules dissolved in 1 teaspoon boiling water brown food colouring
cocoa powder, for dusting

FILLING
1 quantity Vanilla Cream (see page 28)
1 teaspoon coffee extract

2 solid baking sheets, lined with baking parchment
a piping bag, fitted with a plain tip

MAKES 20

Prepare the Basic Macarons mixture according to the recipe on page 6, adding the coffee extract and brown food colouring to the meringue mixture in Step 4.

Pipe rounds of mixture onto the prepared baking sheets. Tap the baking sheets sharply on the work surface, then lightly dust cocoa powder over the tops. Leave the macarons to rest for 15 minutes–1 hour.

Preheat the oven to 170°C (325°F) Gas 3.

Bake the macarons in the preheated oven, one sheet at a time, for 10 minutes. Leave to cool on the baking sheet.

To make the filling, prepare the Vanilla Cream according to the recipe on page 28 and stir in the coffee extract. Fill the piping bag with the coffee cream and pipe it onto half the macaron shells. Pipe two or three layers of filling to make an extra-generous filling. Sandwich with the other half of the shells and leave to rest for about 30 minutes before serving.

Caramel, nuts & spice

Salted caramel

Salted caramel seems to be the flavour of the moment, and the combination works like a dream sandwiched in the middle of crisp and melt-in-the-mouth macarons.

1 quantity Basic Macarons recipe (see page 6)
1 teaspoon vanilla extract

FILLING
75 g/⅓ cup caster/ superfine sugar
75 g/⅓ cup light muscovado/light brown sugar
50 g/3 tablespoons unsalted butter
100 ml/½ cup double/ heavy cream
½ teaspoon sea salt flakes

2 solid baking sheets, lined with baking parchment

MAKES 20

Prepare the Basic Macarons mixture according to the recipe on page 6, adding the vanilla extract to the meringue mixture in Step 4.

Pipe rounds of mixture onto the prepared baking sheets. Tap the baking sheets sharply on the work surface and leave the macarons to rest for 15 minutes–1 hour.

Preheat the oven to 170°C (325°F) Gas 3.

Bake the macarons in the preheated oven, one sheet at a time, for 10 minutes. Leave to cool on the baking sheet.

To make the filling, put the caster/superfine sugar and 2 tablespoons water in a small saucepan over low heat and let the sugar dissolve completely. Bring to the boil, then cook until the syrup turns to an amber-coloured caramel. Remove from the heat and add the muscovado/brown sugar, butter and cream. Stir to dissolve, then return to the low heat and simmer for 3–4 minutes, until the caramel has thickened and will coat the back of a spoon. Remove from the heat, add the salt, pour into a bowl and leave until completely cold and thick.

Spread the filling over half the macaron shells and sandwich with the other half. Leave to rest for about 30 minutes before serving.

Banoffee

For this grown-up version of the family favourite, bananas, caramel, chocolate and cream compete in a divine filling.

1 quantity Basic Macarons
  recipe (see page 6)
yellow food colouring
2–3 tablespoons finely
  chopped dried banana
  chips

FILLING
75 g/⅓ cup caster/
  superfine sugar
1 large or 2 small, ripe
  bananas, peeled and
  thickly sliced
100 ml/½ cup double/
  heavy cream
½ quantity Dark
  Chocolate Ganache
  (see page 30)

2 solid baking sheets, lined
  with baking parchment
a piping bag, fitted with
  a plain tip

MAKES 20

Prepare the Basic Macarons mixture according to the recipe on page 6, adding yellow food colouring to the meringue mixture in Step 4.

Pipe rounds of mixture onto the prepared baking sheets. Tap the baking sheets sharply on the work surface, then scatter the chopped banana chips over the tops. Leave the macarons to rest for 15 minutes–1 hour.

Preheat the oven to 170°C (325°F) Gas 3.

Bake the macarons in the preheated oven, one sheet at a time, for 10 minutes. Leave to cool on the baking sheet.

To make the filling, put the sugar and 1–2 tablespoons water in a small saucepan over low heat and let the sugar dissolve completely. Increase the heat and bring to the boil, then cook until the syrup turns to an amber-coloured caramel. Remove from the heat and add the sliced bananas. Stir to coat and soften in the caramel. Tip the contents of the pan into a food processor and blend until smooth, then set aside to cool completely.

Lightly whip the cream. Spread the Dark Chocolate Ganache onto half the macaron shells. Fill the piping bag with the whipped cream and pipe a circle of it onto the remaining macaron shells, then spoon the banoffee sauce into the middle. Sandwich the macarons together and leave to rest for about 30 minutes before serving.

Caramel & nutmeg ganache

Look for edible gold sugar stars at sugarcraft suppliers (see page 144) to scatter liberally over the top of these macarons – perfect for the festive season.

1 quantity Basic Macarons
  recipe (see page 6)
brown food colouring
freshly grated nutmeg
edible gold stars

FILLING
75 g/⅓ cup caster/
  superfine sugar
200 ml/¾ cup double/
  heavy cream
150 g/5 oz. dark/
  bittersweet chocolate,
  finely chopped
¼ teaspoon freshly
  grated nutmeg

*2 solid baking sheets, lined
  with baking parchment*

MAKES 20

Prepare the filling before making the macaron shells.

Put the sugar and 1 tablespoon water in a small saucepan over low–medium heat and let the sugar dissolve completely. Increase the heat and bring to the boil, then cook until the syrup turns to an amber-coloured caramel. Remove the pan from the heat and pour in the cream. Stir until smooth, returning to a low heat if necessary to re-melt the caramel.

Tip the chopped chocolate into a heatproof bowl, pour the hot caramel cream over it, add the nutmeg and stir until smooth. Leave to cool, then cover and refrigerate until needed.

Prepare the Basic Macarons mixture according to the recipe on page 6, adding brown food colouring and a generous grating of nutmeg to the meringue mixture in Step 4.

Pipe rounds of mixture onto the prepared baking sheets. Tap the baking sheets sharply on the work surface, then scatter gold stars over the tops. Leave the macarons to rest for 15 minutes–1 hour.

Preheat the oven to 170°C (325°F) Gas 3.

Bake the macarons in the preheated oven, one sheet at a time, for 10 minutes. Leave to cool on the baking sheet.

Spread the filling over half the macaron shells and sandwich with the other half. Leave to rest for about 30 minutes before serving.

Peanut butter & jelly

An iconic sandwich filling has inspired these little macarons – it shouldn't work but somehow it does! The homemade peanut butter really does make all the difference here.

2 tablespoons shelled, skinned and unsalted peanuts
1 quantity Basic Macarons recipe (see page 6)
extra peanuts, finely chopped, for sprinkling
pink sugar sprinkles

FILLING
75 g/½ cup shelled, skinned and unsalted peanuts
1 tablespoon icing/confectioners' sugar
3 tablespoons sweetened condensed milk
2 tablespoons unsalted butter
a pinch of salt
4 tablespoons raspberry jam/jelly

2 solid baking sheets, lined with baking parchment

MAKES ABOUT 30

Very finely chop the peanuts in a food processor.

Prepare the Basic Macarons mixture according to the recipe on page 6, adding the finely chopped peanuts to the food processor in Step 1.

Pipe 2.5-cm/1-inch rounds of mixture onto the prepared baking sheets. Tap the baking sheets sharply on the work surface, then sprinkle the finely chopped peanuts over the tops of half the macaron shells and sugar sprinkles over the other half. Leave the macarons to rest for 15 minutes–1 hour.

Preheat the oven to 170°C (325°F) Gas 3.

Bake the macarons in the preheated oven, one sheet at a time, for 7 minutes. Leave to cool on the baking sheet. Leave the oven on.

To make the filling, put the peanuts in a roasting pan and toast in the oven for 5 minutes, or until golden. Remove from the oven and leave to cool for 2–3 minutes before finely chopping in the food processor. Add the sugar, condensed milk, butter and salt and pulse again until the mixture turns to peanut butter.

Spread the peanut butter onto half the macaron shells. Spread the raspberry jam/jelly onto the remaining macaron shells and sandwich the two together. Leave to rest for 30 minutes before serving.

Almond praline

I love caramel in all its forms, and when mixed with almonds, it's a match made in heaven. Add whipped cream and you've got yourself a very delicious macaron.

1 quantity Basic Macarons recipe (see page 6)
2 tablespoons slivered almonds, chopped
1 tablespoon icing/confectioners' sugar

FILLING
50 g/⅓ cup blanched almonds
50 g/¼ cup caster/superfine sugar
125 ml/½ cup double/heavy cream

3 solid baking sheets

MAKES 20

Prepare the filling before you make the macaron shells. Preheat the oven to 180°C (350°F) Gas 4. Line 2 baking sheets with parchment paper and oil the third sheet with sunflower oil.

Tip the blanched almonds into a small roasting pan and toast in the preheated oven for about 5 minutes. Leave to cool slightly.

Put the sugar and 1 tablespoon water in a small saucepan over low–medium heat and let the sugar dissolve completely. Increase the heat and bring to the boil, then cook until the syrup turns to an amber-coloured caramel. Add the toasted almonds and, working quickly, stir to coat in the caramel. Tip the praline mixture onto the oiled baking sheet and leave until completely cold. Break the cold, hard praline into pieces and whiz in the food processor until finely ground. Store in an airtight container until ready to use.

Prepare the Basic Macarons mixture according to the recipe on page 6.

Pipe rounds of mixture onto the lined baking sheets. Tap the baking sheets sharply on the work surface, then scatter the chopped slivered almonds and icing/confectioners' sugar over the tops. Leave the macarons to rest for 15 minutes–1 hour.

Preheat the oven to 170°C (325°F) Gas 3.

Bake the macarons in the preheated oven, one sheet at a time, for 10 minutes. Leave to cool on the baking sheet. Lightly whip the cream and stir in the ground praline. Spread the filling over half the macaron shells and sandwich with the other half. Leave to rest for 30 minutes before serving.

Hazelnut & chocolate

These mini-macarons are filled with a homemade chocolate and hazelnut spread – an altogether more sophisticated version of the storebought variety.

1 quantity Basic Macarons recipe (see page 6, but follow instructions in method, right)

50 g/⅓ cup ground hazelnuts

1 tablespoon cocoa powder

FILLING

35 g/¼ cup blanched hazelnuts

4 tablespoons sweetened condensed milk

50 g/2 oz. dark/ bittersweet chocolate, finely chopped

1 tablespoon double/ heavy cream

a pinch of salt

2 solid baking sheets, lined with baking parchment

MAKES ABOUT 30

Prepare the filling before you make the macaron shells. Preheat the oven to 180°C (350°F) Gas 4. Line 2 baking sheets with parchment paper and oil the third sheet with sunflower oil.

Tip the blanched almonds into a small roasting pan and toast in the preheated oven for about 5 minutes. Leave to cool slightly.

Put the sugar and 1 tablespoon water in a small saucepan over low–medium heat and let the sugar dissolve completely. Increase the heat and bring to the boil, then cook until the syrup turns to an amber-coloured caramel. Add the toasted almonds and, working quickly, stir to coat in the caramel. Tip the praline mixture onto the oiled baking sheet and leave until completely cold. Break the cold, hard praline into pieces and whizz in the food processor until finely ground. Store in an airtight container until ready to use.

Prepare the Basic Macarons mixture according to the recipe on page 6.

Pipe rounds of mixture onto the lined baking sheets. Tap the baking sheets sharply on the work surface, then scatter the chopped slivered almonds and icing/confectioners' sugar over the tops. Leave the macarons to rest for 15 minutes–1 hour.

Preheat the oven to 170°C (325°F) Gas 3.

Bake the macarons in the preheated oven, one sheet at a time, for 10 minutes. Leave to cool on the baking sheet. Lightly whip the cream and stir in the ground praline. Spread the filling over half the macaron shells and sandwich with the other half. Leave to rest for 30 minutes before serving.

Gingerbread spice

Here are all the flavours of Christmas in one crisp mouthful. Warm spices and caramel are combined in a macaron that's somewhat similar to gingerbread.

1 quantity Basic Macarons recipe (see page 6)
1 teaspoon ground cinnamon
1 teaspoon ground ginger
a pinch of ground cloves
a pinch of freshly grated nutmeg

FILLING
150 g/²⁄₃ cup mascarpone
1 generous tablespoon dulce de leche
1 tablespoon finely chopped stem ginger
½ teaspoon ground cinnamon

2 solid baking sheets, lined with baking parchment

MAKES 20

Prepare the Basic Macarons mixture according to the recipe on page 6, adding the cinnamon, ginger, cloves and nutmeg to the food processor in Step 1.

Pipe rounds of mixture onto the prepared baking sheets. Tap the baking sheets sharply on the work surface and leave the macarons to rest for 15 minutes–1 hour.

Preheat the oven to 170°C (325°F) Gas 3.

Bake the macarons in the preheated oven, one sheet at a time, for 10 minutes. Leave to cool on the baking sheet.

To make the filling, put the mascarpone in a small bowl and stir in the dulce de leche, stem ginger and cinnamon.

Spread the filling over half the macaron shells and sandwich with the other half. Leave to rest for about 30 minutes before serving.

Decorated macarons

Say it with macarons! Beautiful and imaginative macarons to give as gifts, for Mother's Day, Father's Day, special birthdays, anniversaries or even to present to your guests as wedding favours – these show-stopping macaron designs will always be greeted with a smile!

Special occasions

Be my Valentine

These beautiful heart-shaped macarons make the perfect treat for Valentine's Day or for any loved one, any day of the year!

SHELLS
1 quantity Patissier's
   Macarons (see page 10)
2.5 g/½ teaspoon pink,
   dusky pink or claret,
   food colouring

FILLING
a drop of rose cordial
½ quantity Buttercream
   (see page 24)

DECORATION
10 g white sugarpaste
purple, yellow or pink
   food colouring
1 quantity Royal Icing
   (see page 20)

1 piping bag fitted with a
   8-mm/⅜-inch round tip
Heart template (see page
   140)
transparent silicone mat
small piping bag for icing
mini flower cutter

MAKES 40

Preheat the oven to 160°C (325°F) Gas 3.

Prepare the Patissier's Macarons mixture according to the recipe on page 10, but add the food colouring in step 4 before folding the egg whites into the dry ingredients. Put the mixture into a piping bag fitted with an 8-mm/⅜-inch tip.

Place the Heart template on a baking sheet and place a silicone mat on top. Pipe 80 hearts, using the template as a guide. Tap the bottom of the sheet lightly on the work surface. Carefully slide the template out from under the silicone mat. Leave the macarons to rest for 15–30 minutes.

Bake the macarons, in the preheated oven for 8 minutes, until the tops are crisp, and the undersides are dry. Leave to cool for 30 minutes on the baking sheet. Leave the oven on.

For the filling, mix the rose cordial into the Buttercream. Line the macarons in pairs. Fill one half of the shells with Buttercream, then sandwich the macarons together gently. Leave to set in the fridge for 12 hours before serving.

Use a toothpick to add some food colouring to the sugarpaste. Knead until the colour is even. Roll out and use the mini flower cutter to cut out flowers. Leave to dry before use.

Use a toothpick to add some food colouring to the royal icing. Transfer to a small piping bag for icing, and snip off the end to create a small hole. Pipe dots onto the macarons, then use the icing to stick the flowers onto them. Leave to dry for 1 hour.

Mother's Day floral bouquet

This bouquet of macaron flowers makes an ideal gift for Mother's Day. Make them in either pink or green, fill them with rose and green tea buttercreams and hand paint them with flowers.

SHELLS

1 quantity Patissier's Macarons (see page 10)

3 g/½ teaspoon pink or gooseberry food colouring

FILLING

1½ tablespoons rose cordial

1 teaspoon green tea powder

1 quantity Buttercream (see page 27)

2 piping bags fitted with 1-cm/½-inch round tips

5.5-cm/2¼-inch round template (see page 140)

DECORATION

pink and green food colouring paints

1 fine paintbrush
1 flat paintbrush
transparent silicone mat
4-cm/1½-inch round template (see page 140)

MAKES 40

Preheat the oven to 160°C (325°F) Gas 3.

Prepare the Patissier's Macarons mixture according to the recipe on page 10, but add the food colouring before folding the egg whites into the dry ingredients. Put the mixture into a piping bag fitted with a 1-cm/½-inch round tip.

Place the 5.5-cm/2¼-inch round template on a baking sheet, and place a silicone mat on top. Pipe 40 rounds, using the template as a guide. (You may need more than one baking sheet.) Tap the bottom of the sheets lightly on the work surface. Carefully slide the template out from under the silicone mat. Leave the macarons to rest for 15–30 minutes.

Bake the macarons, in the preheated oven for 8 minutes, until the tops are crisp and the undersides are dry. Leave to cool for 30 minutes on the baking sheet. Leave the oven on.

For the fillings, mix the rose cordial into half of the Buttercream and the green tea into the other half.

Line the macarons in pairs. Fill one quarter of the shells with rose Buttercream and the rest with green tea buttercream, then sandwich the macarons together gently. Leave to set in the fridge for 12 hours before serving.

Prepare the food colouring paints according the the package instructions. Use a clean, flat paintbrush to paint flowers onto the tops of the macarons. Use a fine paintbrush to paint stems and detail. Leave to dry for 1 hour.

Sweet sixteen treats

Cute as cherry pie – these dainty little pink and white macarons with a cherry jam/jelly and lychee filling make the perfect treat to serve at any Sweet Sixteen party.

SHELLS
2 quantities Patissier's Macarons (see page 10)
3 g/²⁄₃ teaspoon baby pink food colouring

FILLING
a few drops rose cordial, to taste
200 g/generous ½ cup cherry jam/jelly
400-g/14-oz. can lychees in syrup, drained and chopped

DECORATION
pink and green food colouring paints

transparent silicone mat
5-cm/2-inch round templates (see page 140)
2 piping bags fitted with 1-cm/½-inch round tips
2 fine paintbrushes

MAKES 40

Preheat the oven to 160°C (325°F) Gas 3.

Prepare the first quantity of Patissier's Macarons mixture according to the recipe on page 10. No food colouring is added to this batch. Put the mixture into a piping bag fitted with a 1-cm/½-inch round tip.

Place the 5-cm/2-inch round template on a baking sheet, and place a silicone mat on top. Pipe 40 rounds onto the silicone mat, using the template as a guide. (You will need more than one baking sheet.) Tap the bottom of the sheets lightly. Carefully slide the template out from under the silicone mat. Leave the macarons to rest for 15–30 minutes.

Bake the macarons, one sheet at a time, in the preheated oven for 8 minutes, until the tops are crisp and the undersides are dry. Leave to cool for 30 minutes on the baking sheet. Leave the oven on.

Meanwhile, prepare the second quantity of Patissier's Macarons mixture according to the recipe on page 10, but add the baby pink food colouring before folding the egg whites into the dry ingredients. Pipe and bake this second batch following the method given for the first batch.

To make the filling, add the rose cordial to the cherry jam/jelly, then mix in the chopped lychees.

Spread a teaspoonful of the filling onto the flat-sides of each pink shell, then top with the white shells, and press together gently. Leave to set in the fridge for 12 hours before serving.

Prepare the food colouring paints. Use paintbrushes to paint cherries on each white shell. Leave to dry for 1 hour.

Jewelled birthday crown

A wonderful addition to any birthday, a golden crown instantly renders the recipient royalty for their special day! Why not display as part of a celebratory table setting?

SHELLS
1 quantity Patissier's Macarons (see page 10)
3 g/²⁄₃ teaspoon autumn leaf food colouring

FILLING
1 quantity Caramel Chocolate Ganache (see page 28)

DECORATION
1 quantity Royal Icing (see page 20)
autumn leaf food colouring
40 1-cm/½-inch sugar diamond stones
edible gold lustre spray

piping bag fitted with a 1-cm/½-inch round tip
5-cm/2-inch round template (see page 140)
transparent silicone mat
small piping bag for icing

MAKES 40

Preheat the oven to 160°C (325°F) Gas 3.

Prepare the Patissier's Macarons mixture according to the recipe on page 10, but add the autumn leaf food colouring before folding the egg whites into the dry ingredients. Put the mixture into a piping bag fitted with a 1-cm/½-inch round tip.

Place the 5 cm/2-inch round template on a baking sheet, and place a silicone mat on top. Pipe 80 round macarons onto the silicone mat, using the template as a guide. (You may need more than one baking sheet.)

Tap the bottom of the sheet lightly on the work surface. Carefully slide the template out from under the silicone mat. Leave the macarons to rest for 15–30 minutes.

Bake the macarons, one sheet at a time, in the preheated oven for 8 minutes, until the tops are crisp and the undersides are dry. Leave to cool for 30 minutes on the baking sheet.

Place the macaron shells in two rows. Spread the Salted Caramel Ganache filling onto the flat-sides of half the shells and top with the remaining shells, pressing them together gently. Leave to set in the fridge for 12 hours before serving.

Spray the shells with the edible gold lustre. Using a toothpick and a little Royal Icing, stick a sugar diamond stone in the centre of each macaron.

Use a cocktail stick/toothpick to add a little autumn leaf food colouring to the remaining Royal Icing and, using the small piping bag for icing, pipe tiny dots around the diamonds. Leave to dry for 1 hour.

Father's Day black & gold

Striking and a little bit James Bond, these sleek black shells, brushed with a gold and filled with apricot ganache, make a stylish gift for Father's Day or add glamour to any cocktail party.

SHELLS
1 quantity Patissier's Macarons (see page 10)
2.5 g/½ teaspoon extra black food colouring

FILLING
1 ready-to-eat dried apricot, finely chopped
½ quantity White Chocolate Ganache (see page 23)
tangerine/apricot food colouring

DECORATION
gold food colouring powder
rejuvenating spirit, to dilute the powder

5-cm/2-inch round template (see page 140)
transparent silicone mat
2 piping bags fitted with 1-cm/½-inch round tips
flat paintbrush

MAKES 30

Preheat the oven to 160°C (325°F) Gas 3.

Prepare the Patissier's Macarons mixture according to the recipe on page 10, but add the extra black food colouring before folding the egg whites into the dry ingredients. Put the mixture into a piping bag fitted with a 1-cm/½-inch round tip.

Place the 5-cm/2-inch round template on a baking sheet, and place a silicone mat on top. Pipe 60 macarons onto the silicone mat, using the template as a guide. (You may need more than one baking sheet.)

Tap the bottom of the sheet lightly on the work surface. Carefully slide the template out from under the silicone mat. Leave the macarons to rest for 15–30 minutes.

Bake the macarons, one sheet at a time, in the preheated oven for 8 minutes, until the tops are crisp and the undersides are dry. Leave to cool for 30 minutes on the baking sheet. Leave the oven on.

For the filling, mix the chopped dried apricot into the ganache and use a toothpick to add tangerine food colour. Mix until desired colour is achieved.

Place the macaron shells in pairs. Spread the filling onto the flat-sides of half the shells and top with the remaining shells, pressing them together gently. Leave to set in the fridge for 12 hours before serving.

Add the rejuvenating spirit to the gold food colouring powder and, using the paintbrush, paint the tops of the macarons with straight upward strokes. Leave to dry for 1 hour.

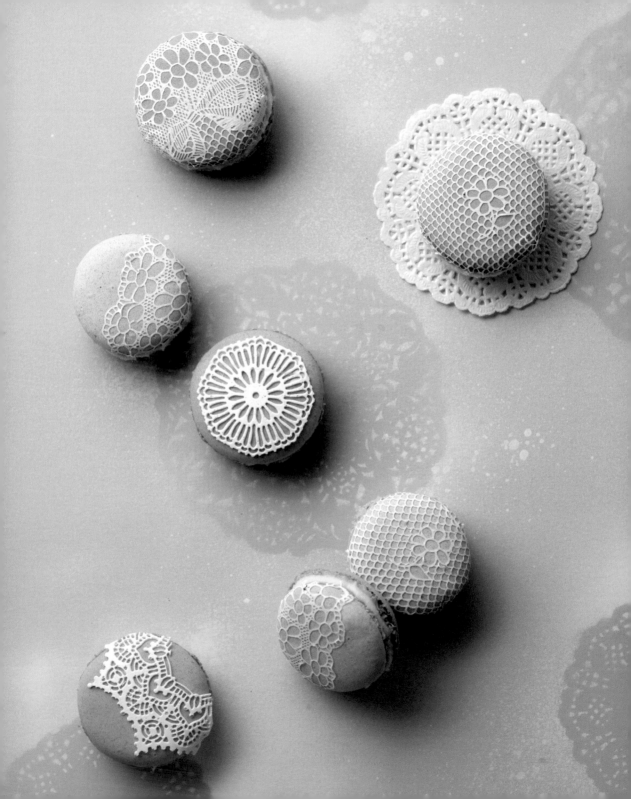

Something blue ...

This ingenious lace icing (see page 22) makes the ultimate macaron to give to your guests as a wedding favour when presented in a box or gift bag. Change the colour to suit your own theme if wished.

SHELLS
1 quantity Patissier's
  Macarons (see page 10)
3 g/2⁄3 teaspoon royal
  blue food colouring

FILLING
1 quantity Buttercream
  (see page 27)
2 tablespoons mango
  purée
20 g/¾ oz. dried mango,
  finely chopped

DECORATATION
lace effect kit (see page 144)
piping bag fitted with a
  1-cm/½-inch round tip
5-cm/2-inch round template
  (see page 140)
transparent silicone mat

MAKES 40

Preheat the oven to 160°C (325°F) Gas 3.

Prepare the Patissier's Macarons mixture according to the recipe on page 10, but add the royal blue food colouring before folding the egg whites into the dry ingredients. Put the mixture into a piping bag fitted with a 1-cm/½-inch round tip.

Place the 5-cm/2-inch round template on a baking sheet, and place a silicone mat on top. Pipe 80 round macarons onto the silicone mat, using the template as a guide. (You may need more than one baking sheet.)

Tap the bottom of the sheet lightly on the work surface. Carefully slide the template out from under the silicone mat. Leave the macarons to rest for 15–30 minutes.

Bake the macarons, one sheet at a time, in the preheated oven for 8 minutes, until the tops are crisp and the undersides are dry. Leave to cool for 30 minutes on the baking sheet.

For the filling, combine the mango purée and dried mango into the Buttercream.

Place the macaron shells in two rows. Spread the filling onto the flat-sides of half the shells and top with the remaining shells, pressing them together gently. Leave to set in the frdge for 12 hours before serving.

To decorate, follow the instructions for creating a sugar lace effect on page 22.

Precious gems

Semi-precious stones adorn these crisp and fresh peppermint-filled macarons. This design works beautifully as an anniversary gift as you can adapt the gem to suit the number of years being celebrated.

SHELLS
1 quantity Patissier's
    Macarons
(see page 10)
3 g/²⁄₃ teaspoon teal food
    colouring

FILLING
1 quantity Buttercream
    (see page 27)
a few drops peppermint
    essence oil, to taste

DECORATION
1 quantity Royal Icing
    (see page 20)
1-cm/½-inch pink sugar
    diamond stones
1 small can of edible pearl
    lustre shimmer spray
20 g/¾ oz. sugar pearls

piping bag fitted with a
    1-cm/½-inch round tip
5-cm/2-inch round template
    (see page 140)
transparent silicone mat
small piping bag for icing

MAKES 40

Preheat the oven to 160°C (325°F) Gas 3.

Prepare the Patissier's Macarons mixture according to the recipe on page 10, but add the teal food colouring before folding the egg whites into the dry ingredients. Put the mixture into a piping bag fitted with a 1-cm/½-inch round tip.

Place the 5-mm/¼-inch round template on a baking sheet, and place a silicone mat on top. Pipe 80 macarons onto the silicone mat, using the template as a guide. (You may need more than one baking sheet.)

Tap the bottom of the sheet lightly on the work surface. Carefully slide the template out from under the silicone mat. Leave the macarons to rest for 15–30 minutes.

Bake the macarons, one sheet at a time, in the preheated oven for 8 minutes, until the tops are crisp and the undersides are dry. Leave to cool for 30 minutes on the baking sheet.

For the filling, mix the peppermint essence oil to the Buttercream.

Place the macaron shells in two rows. Spread the Buttercream mixture onto the flat-sides of half the shells and top with the remaining shells, pressing them together gently. Leave to set in the fridge for 12 hours before serving.

Spray the shells with the edible pearl lustre. Using a toothpick and a little Royal Icing, stick a pink sugar diamond stone in the centre of each macaron and sugar pearls around them. Leave to dry for 1 hour.

Animal Magic

Teddy bears

These adorable little smiling teddy faces will delight adults and children alike. See page 15 for further guidance on piping their ears.

SHELLS
2 quantities Patissier's
    Macarons (see page 10)
4 g/¾ teaspoon dark
    brown food colouring
2 g/¼ teaspoon chestnut
    food colouring

DECORATION
1 quantity Royal Icing
    (see page 20)
2.5 g/½ teaspoon dark
    brown food colouring
120 sugar pearls

1 piping bag fitted with a
    1-cm/½-inch round tip
2 piping bags fitted with
    6-mm/¼-inch round tips
5-cm/2-inch round template
    (see page 140)
transparent silicone mat
2.5-cm/1-inch round template
    (see page 140)
small piping bag for icing

MAKES 60 TEDDIES

Preheat the oven to 160°C (325°F) Gas 3.

Prepare the first quantity of macaron mixture according to the recipe on page 10, but add the dark brown food colouring before folding the egg whites into the dry ingredients. Put three-quarters of it into a piping bag fitted with a 1-cm/½-inch round tip, and put the rest into a piping bag fitted with a 6-mm/¼-inch round tip.

Place the 5-cm/2-inch round template on a baking sheet, and place a silicone mat on top. Using the piping bag fitted with the 1-cm/½-inch tip, pipe the round faces onto the mat, using the template as a guide. Pipe the ears using the piping bag with the 6-mm/¼-inch tip (see page 15). Repeat to make 60 bears.

Tap the bottom of the sheets lightly on the work surface. Slide the template out from under the mat. Leave to rest for 15–30 minutes. Bake in the preheated oven for 8 minutes. Leave to cool for 30 minutes on the baking sheets. Leave the oven on.

Meanwhile, make the second batch of macaron mixture and follow the instructions above for piping and baking but using the chestnut food colouring, a piping bag fitted with a 6-mm/¼-inch tip and the 2.5-cm/1-inch template.

Add the dark brown food colouring to the royal icing. Transfer to a small piping bag and snip off the end to create a small hole. Use it to fix the noses in place before piping eyes and a mouth. Finally use a little to fix the pearls onto the ears.

Leave to dry for 1 hour before serving.

Sleepy cats

Decide what expression to give the kitties. You can opt for whatever colour you like by experimenting with different food colouring.

SHELLS
3 quantities Patissier's
   Macarons (see page 10)
3 g/²/₃ teaspoon tangerine
   food colouring
8 g/1½ teaspoons dark
   brown food colouring

FILLING
1 quantity Dark Chocolate
   Ganache (see page 23)
1 tablespoon peppermint
   essence oil

DECORATION
20 g/¾ oz. white
   sugarpaste
baby pink food colouring
1 quantity Royal Icing
   (see page 20)
black food colouring

3 piping bags fitted with
   1-cm/½-inch round tips
5-cm/2-inch round template
   (see page 140)
transparent silicone mat
tiny heart and flower cutters
small piping bag for icing

MAKES 30 CATS

Preheat the oven to 160°C (325°F) Gas 3.

Prepare the first quantity of Patissier's Macarons mixture according to the recipe on page 10, but add the tangerine food colouring before folding the egg whites into the dry ingredients. Put the mixture into a piping bag fitted with a 1-cm/½-inch round tip.

Place the 5-cm/2-inch round template on a baking sheet, and place a silicone mat on top. Pipe 30 rounds onto the silicone mat, using the template as a guide. Using a toothpick, drag and pull the ears from the round faces (for further guidance see page 15).

Tap the bottom of the sheets lightly on the work surface. Slide the template out from under the mat. Leave the macarons to rest for 15–30 minutes. Bake the macarons, one sheet at a time, in the preheated oven for 8 minutes, until the tops are crisp and the undersides are dry. Leave to cool for 30 minutes on the baking sheets. Leave the oven on.

Meanwhile, prepare the second and third batches of Patissier's Macarons according to the recipe on page 10, but add half of the dark brown food colouring to each batch before folding in the egg whites. Pipe and bake 90 brown macaron shells repeating the process above.

Mix the peppermint essence oil into the Ganache. Put the Ganache into a piping bag with 1-cm/½-inch tip. Line the brown macarons into rows of 3. Pipe some Ganache onto the first two shells, and stack them into towers with the third, empty, shell on top. Repeat to make 30. Leave to set in the fridge for 12 hours before finishing.

Use a toothpick to add a little baby pink or orange food colouring to the white sugarpaste. Knead until the colour is even, then roll out to a thickness of 3 mm/⅛ inch. Cut out hearts and flowers and leave to dry. Make the Royal Icing recipe and use a toothpick to add black food colouring to create a dark shade. Transfer to a small piping bag for icing, and snip off the end to create a small hole. Pipe on whiskers, eyes and noses. Allow to dry for 20 minutes.

Use the rest of the icing to stick on the hearts and flowers, then to stick the faces to the bodies. Leave to dry for 1 hour before serving.

Three little piggies

Using two different sizes of macaron gives you the effect of having a head and body of an animal, as shown here with these cute pigs.

SHELLS
2 quantities Patissier's Macarons (see page 10)
2.5 g/½ teaspoon dusky pink food colouring
3 g/⅔ teaspoon pink food colouring

FILLING
1 quantity Buttercream (see page 27)
3 tablespoons strawberry jam/jelly, sieved/strained

DECORATION
baby pink food colouring
30 g/1 oz white sugarpaste
1 quantity Royal Icing (see page 20)
black food colouring

2 piping bags fitted with 1-cm/½-inch round tips
5.5-cm/2¼-inch round template (see page 140)
transparent silicone mat
4-cm/1½-inch round template (see page 140)
small piping bag for icing

MAKES 40 PIGS

Preheat the oven to 160°C (325°F) Gas 3.

Prepare the first quantity of Patissier's Macarons mixture according to the recipe on page 10, but add the dusky pink food colouring before folding the egg whites into the dry ingredients. Put the mixture into a piping bag fitted with a 1-cm/½-inch round tip.

Place the 5.5-cm/2¼-inch round template on a baking sheet, and place a silicone mat on top. Pipe 80 rounds onto the mat, using the template as a guide. (You will need more than one baking sheet.) Tap the bottom of the sheets lightly on the work surface. Slide the template out from under the mat. Leave the macarons to rest for 15–30 minutes.

Bake the macarons, one sheet at a time, in the preheated oven for 8 minutes, until the tops are crisp and the undersides are dry. Leave to cool for 30 minutes on the baking sheets. Leave the oven on.

Meanwhile, prepare the second quantity of Patissier's Macarons mixture according to the recipe on page 10, but add the pink food colouring before folding the egg whites into the dry ingredients. Put the mixture a piping bag fitted with a 1-cm/½-inch round tip. Pipe and bake 40 rounds as above but using the 4-cm/1½-inch template.

Use a toothpick to add some baby pink food colouring to the white sugarpaste. Knead until the colour is even. Shape the sugarpaste into the pigs' noses, ears and tails. Leave to dry before use.

To make the filling, mix the jam/jelly into the Buttercream. Line the dusky pink macarons into rows of 2, flat-side up. Using a teaspoon, place a little filling mixture onto half of the dusky pink shells, and sandwich the pairs together gently to create 40 macarons. Leave to set in the fridge for at least 12 hours before finishing.

Make the Royal Icing recipe and use a toothpick to add black food colouring to create a dark shade. Transfer to a small piping bag for icing and snip off the end to create a small hole. Pipe eyes and mouths on the smaller pink shells and allow to dry for 20 minutes. Use the rest of the icing to stick the faces onto the dusky pink bodies, then to attach the ears, noses and tails. Leave to dry for 1 hour before serving.

Crawling caterpillar

These cheerful caterpillars are easier to make than they look — see page 17 for guidance on piping these fun joined macarons.

SHELLS
2 quantities Patissier's Macarons (see page 10)
3.5 g/generous ⅔ teaspoon gooseberry food colouring
3 g/⅔ teaspoon tangerine food colouring

FILLING
3 tablespoons passion fruit jam/jelly
1 quantity Dark Chocolate Ganache (see page 30)

DECORATION
1 quantity Royal Icing (see page 20)
black food colouring

piping bag fitted with a 1-cm/½-inch round tip
Caterpillar template (see page 140)
transparent silicone mat
Caterpillar Legs template (see page 140)
piping bag fitted with a 4-mm/⅛-inch round tip
2 small piping bags for icing

MAKES 20 CATERPILLARS

Preheat the oven to 160°C (325°F) Gas 3.

Prepare the first quantity of Patissier's Macarons mixture according to the recipe on page 10, but add the gooseberry food colouring before folding the egg whites into the dry ingredients. Put the mixture into a piping bag fitted with a 1-cm/½-inch round tip.

Place the Caterpillar template on a baking sheet, and place a silicone mat on top. Pipe 40 caterpillars, using the template as a guide. (You will need more than one baking sheet.) Tap the bottom of the sheets lightly on the work surface. Slide the template out from under the mat. Leave the macarons to rest for 15–30 minutes.

Bake the macarons, one sheet at a time, in the preheated oven for 8 minutes, until the tops are crisp and the undersides are dry. Leave to cool for 30 minutes on the baking sheet. Leave the oven on.

Meanwhile, prepare the second quantity of Patissier's Macarons mixture according to the recipe on page 10, but add the tangerine food colouring before folding the egg whites into the dry ingredients. Put the mixture into a piping bag fitted with a 4-mm/⅛-inch round tip.

Using the Caterpillar Legs template and following the method above, pipe, rest and bake 80 small shells.

To make the filling, mix the jam/jelly into the Ganache. Spread filling onto the flat-side of one caterpillar shell and sandwich together with another. Repeat with the remaining shells. Leave to set in the fridge for at least 12 hours before finishing.

Make the Royal Icing and divide it into two portions. Use a toothpick to add black food colouring to one portion to create a dark shade. Transfer to a small piping bag for icing and snip off the end to create a small hole. Repeat with the white portion in another small piping bag for icing.

With the black icing, pipe eyes and mouths onto each caterpillar. Use the white icing to stick 4 legs onto each caterpillar, and then to pipe a white spot onto each eye. Finally, use the black icing again pipe a final tiny dot onto each eye. Leave to dry for 1 hour before serving.

Buzzy bees

A honey buttercream is used to fill these cute macarons. Whatever the filling, these buzzy bees are a delight to look at and eat.

SHELLS
1 quantity Patissier's Macarons (see page 10)
3 g/²⁄₃ teaspoon egg yellow food colouring

FILLING
1 quantity Buttercream (see page 27)
3 tablespoons honey

DECORATION
1 quantity Royal Icing (see page 20)
black food colouring

piping bag fitted with a 1-cm/½-inch round tip
6-cm/2³⁄₈-inch round template (see page 140)
small piping bag for icing

MAKES 30 BEES

Preheat the oven to 160°C (325°F) Gas 3.

Prepare the Patissier's Macarons mixture according to the recipe on page 10, but add the egg yellow food colouring before folding the egg whites into the dry ingredients. Put the mixture into a piping bag fitted with a 1-cm/½-inch round tip.

Place the 6-cm/2³⁄₈-inch round template on a baking sheet, and place a silicone mat on top. Pipe 60 rounds, using the template as a guide. (You will need more than one baking sheet.) Tap the bottom of the sheets lightly on the work surface. Slide the template out from under the mat. Leave the macarons to rest for 15–30 minutes.

Bake the macarons, one sheet at a time, in the preheated oven for 8 minutes, until the tops are crisp and the undersides are dry. Leave to cool for 30 minutes on the baking sheet.

To make the filling, mix the honey into the Buttercream. Spread a teaspoonful of the filling mixture onto the flat-sides of half of the shells, and top with the remaining macaron shells, pressing together gently. Leave to set in the fridge for at least 12 hours before finishing.

Prepare the Royal Icing and use a toothpick to add enough black food colouring to create a dark shade. Transfer to a small piping bag for icing and snip off the end to create a small hole. Pipe 3 lines across each macaron, as well as eyes and a tail. Leave to dry for 1 hour before serving.

Bouncing bunnies

Here's an irresistible idea for the child in all of us! You can make these cute little rabbits for a children's party or spring celebration.

SHELLS
1 quantity Patissier's
   Macarons (see page 10)
3 g/⅔ teaspoon autumn
   leaf food colouring

FILLING
3 tablespoons strawberry
   jam/jelly
1 quantity Buttercream
   (see page 27)

DECORATION
20 g/¾ oz. white
   sugarpaste
baby pink food colouring
orange food colouring
edible gold lustre paint
1 quantity Royal Icing
   (see page 20)
black food colouring
brown food colouring
red (nonpareil) sprinkles

2 piping bags fitted with
   1-cm/½-inch round tips
5-cm/2-inch round template
   (see page 138)
small paintbrush
2 small piping bags for icing
tiny flower cutters

MAKES 40 BUNNIES

Preheat the oven to 160°C (325°F) Gas 3.

Prepare the Patissier's Macarons mixture according to the recipe on page 10, but add the autumn leaf food colouring before folding the egg whites into the dry ingredients. Put the mixture into a piping bag fitted with a 1-cm/½-inch round tip.

Place the 5-cm/2-inch round template on a baking sheet, and place a silicone mat on top. Pipe 40 rounds, using the template as a guide. (You will need more than one baking sheet.) Add ears to 20 of the rounds (see page 15 further guidance on piping ears). Tap the bottom of the sheets lightly on the work surface. Slide the template out from under the mat. Leave the macarons to rest for 15–30 minutes.

Bake the macarons, one sheet at a time, in the preheated oven for 8 minutes, until the tops are crisp and the undersides are dry. Leave to cool for 30 minutes on the baking sheet.

Divide the sugarpaste into two portions. Knead baby pink food colouring into one portion and orange food colouring into the other. Roll out both colours and use a cutter to stamp out flowers. Leave to dry before use.

To make the filling, mix the jam/jelly into the Buttercream. Put the Buttercream into a piping bag fitted with a 1-cm/½-inch round tip. Pipe a little filling onto the flat-sides of all the round macarons, and top with the faces, pressing together gently. Leave to set from at least 12 hours before finishing.

First use a small paintbrush to add a stroke of gold lustre paint down the centre of all the ears. Prepare the Royal Icing, and place one-third of the mixture into a separate bowl. Use a toothpick to add black food colouring to the small portion and brown food colouring to the large portion. Transfer both portions to small piping bags for icing and snip off the ends to create small holes. Pipe black eyes then pipe brown whiskers, and use the brown icing to pipe noses and add a tiny blob at the base of each right ear. Stick some red sprinkles onto each nose, and a flower onto the ear. Leave to dry for 1 hour before serving.

Pudgy pandas

Here a clever stacking effect is used to create an unmistakable black and white panda. It is very simple but extremely effective, and can be used for other animals too – just use your own imagination!

SHELLS
3 quantities Patissier's Macarons (see page 10)
5 g/1 teaspoon black food colouring

FILLING
1 quantity Buttercream (see page 27)
3 tablespoons lemon curd

DECORATION
1 quantity Royal Icing (see page 20)
black food colouring

3 piping bags fitted with 1-cm/½-inch round tips
5-cm/2-inch round template (see page 140)
small piping bag for icing

MAKES 40 PANDAS

Preheat the oven to 160°C (325°F) Gas 3.

Prepare the first quantity of Patissier's Macarons mixture according to the recipe on page 10, but add the black food colouring before folding the egg whites into the dry ingredients. Put the mixture into a piping bag fitted with a 1-cm/½-inch round tip.

Place the 5-cm/2-inch round template on a baking sheet, and place a silicone mat on top. Pipe 40 rounds, using the template as a guide. (You will need more than one baking sheet.) Tap the bottom of the sheets lightly on the work surface. Slide the template out from under the mat. Leave the macarons to rest for 15–30 minutes.

Bake the macarons, one sheet at a time, in the preheated oven for 8 minutes, until the tops are crisp and the undersides are dry. Leave to cool for 30 minutes on the baking sheet. Leave the oven on.

Meanwhile, prepare the second and third quantities of Patissier's Macarons mixture according to the recipe on page 10. No food colouring is added to these batches. Put the mixtures into 2 piping bags fitted with 1-cm/½-inch round tips.

Pipe and bake 80 white macaron shells repeating the process above twice.

To make the filling, mix the lemon curd into the Buttercream.

Spread a teaspoonful of the filling mixture onto the flat-sides of half of the white shells, and top with the black macaron shells, pressing together gently. Leave to set in the fridge for at least 12 hours before finishing.

Make the Royal Icing recipe and use a toothpick to add enough black colouring paste to make a dark shade. Transfer to a small piping bag for icing. Pipe black eyes, noses and ears onto the reserved white macaron shells. Leave to dry for 20 minutes.

Use the remaining icing to stick a face onto the top of each panda's body. Leave to dry for 1 hour before serving.

Playtime

Building blocks

Adding popping candy to the filling just makes these square macarons even more fun and the perfect edible party game!

SHELLS

5 quantities Patissier's Macarons (see page 10)

3 g/²⁄₃ teaspoon dark brown food colouring

5 g/1 teaspoon extra red food colouring

4 g/³⁄₄ teaspoon egg yellow food colouring

3 g/²⁄₃ teaspoon mint green food colouring

4 g/³⁄₄ teaspoon blue food colouring

FILLING

2 quantities Caramel Chocolate Ganache (see page 29)

40 g/1½ oz popping candy

5 piping bags fitted with 6-mm/¼-inch tips

3-cm/1¼-inch square template (see page 139)

transparent silicone mat

MAKES ABOUT 200

Preheat the oven to 160°C (325°F) Gas 3.

Prepare the first quantity of Patissier's Macarons mixture according to the recipe on page 10, but add the gooseberry food colouring before folding the egg whites into the dry ingredients. Put the mixture into a piping bag fitted with a 6-mm/¼-inch round tip.

Place the square template on a baking sheet, and place a silicone mat on top. Pipe the mixture onto the mat, using the template as a guide, filling each square carefully. Carry on until the mixture is used up. (You may need more than one baking sheet.)

Tap the bottom of the sheet lightly on the work surface. Slide the template out from under the mat. Leave the macarons to rest for 15–30 minutes.

Repeat with a further 4 quantities, adding the dark brown, extra red, egg yellow and mint green food colourings before folding the egg whites into the dry ingredients each time.

Bake the macarons, one sheet at a time, in the preheated oven for 6 minutes, until the tops are crisp and the undersides are dry. Leave to cool for 30 minutes on the baking sheet.

Place the macaron shells in pairs of the same colour. Spread some Caramel Chocolate Ganache onto the flat-sides of half the shells, sprinkle with popping candy and top with the remaining shells, pressing them together gently. You will have plenty of building blocks, which will make varying designs depending on how you assemble them. Note: If you don't want to bake this large a quantity, make fewer batches of the mixture, split them at the egg white stage and colour each batch with half the quantity of the food colouring, before folding.

Tetris

Inspired by the addictive 80s puzzle game. They are so pretty and colourful, these joined rows of macarons will enhance any teatime.

SHELLS

4 quantities Patissier's Macarons (see page 10)
4 g/¾ teaspoon gooseberry food colouring
3 g/⅔ teaspoon daffodil yellow food colouring
5 g/1 teaspoon Egyptian orange food colouring
5 g/1 teaspoon rose food colouring
about 150 chocolate chips

FILLING

30 g/2 tablespoons sesame seeds, plus extra to decorate
1 quantity Dark Chocolate Ganache (see page 30)
1 quantity Buttercream (see page 27)
20 g/¾ oz. dried red berries, chopped, plus extra to decorate

4 piping bags fitted with 6-mm/¼-inch tips
Tetris template (see page 141)
transparent silicone mat

MAKES 30 OF EACH

Preheat the oven to 160°C (325°F) Gas 3.

Prepare the first quantity of Patissier's Macarons mixture according to the recipe on page 10, but add the gooseberry food colouring before before folding the egg whites into the dry ingredients. Put the mixture into a piping bag fitted with a 6-mm/¼-inch round tip.

Place the Tetris template on a baking sheet, and place a silicone mat on top. Pipe the macaron mixture onto the mat, using the template as a guide. See page 17 for guidance on piping joined macarons. (You may need more than one baking sheet.)

Tap the bottom of the sheet lightly on the work surface. Slide the template out from under the mat. Leave the macarons to rest for 15–30 minutes.

Repeat the above, using the daffodil yellow, Egyptian orange and rose food colourings.

Sprinkle sesame seeds onto the green row and dried red berries onto the pink row before putting them into the oven. Decorate the orange ones with chocolate chips.

Bake the macarons, one sheet at a time, in the preheated oven for 10 minutes, until the tops are crisp and the undersides are dry. Leave to cool for 30 minutes on the baking sheet.

For the fillings, lightly fry the sesame seeds in a pan and then grind into a paste using a mortar and pestle. Add the sesame paste with a third of the Dark Chocolate Ganache. Place the green macaron shells in two rows. Spread the chocolate sesame mixture onto the flat-sides of half the shells and top with the remaining shells, pressing them together gently. Fill the yellow and orange shells with the remaiing Dark Chocolate Ganache.

Mix the chopped dried berries into the Buttercream, then fill the pink shells with this mixture.

Leave to set in the fridge for at least 12 hours before serving.

Checkers

A game of checkers or draughts will never be the same again – in this version you get to eat each piece you take! The passion fruit adds an extra zing to the Caramel Chocolate Ganache filling.

SHELLS

2 quantities Patissier's Macarons (see page 10)

5 g/1 teaspoon extra black food colouring

5 g/1 teaspoon superwhite icing whitener colouring powder

FILLING

1 quantity Caramel Chocolate Ganache (see page 29)

20 g/¾ oz dried passion fruit, chopped

1 quantity Buttercream (see page 27)

20 fresh raspberries

2 piping bags fitted with 1-cm/½-inch round tips

5-cm/2-inch round template (see page 140)

transparent silicone mat

MAKES 40

Preheat the oven to 160°C (325°F) Gas 3.

Prepare the first quantity of Patissier's Macarons mixture according to the recipe on page 10, but add the extra black food colouring before folding the egg whites into the dry ingredients. Put the mixture into a piping bag fitted with a 1-cm/½-inch round tip.

Place the 5-cm/2-inch round template on a baking sheet, and place a silicone mat on top. Pipe 40 macarons onto the silicone mat, using the template as a guide. (You may need more than one baking sheet.)

Tap the bottom of the sheet lightly on the work surface. Slide the template out from under the mat. Leave the macarons to rest for 15–30 minutes.

Bake the macarons, one sheet at a time, in the preheated oven for 8 minutes, until the tops are crisp and the undersides are dry. Leave to cool for 30 minutes on the baking sheet. Leave the oven on.

Meanwhile, prepare the second quantity of Patissier's Macarons mixture according to the recipe on page 10, but add the superwhite food colouring powder before folding the egg whites into the dry ingredients. Then continue as above.

Add the chopped passion fruit to the Caramel Chocolate Ganache. Place the black shells in two rows. Spread the filling onto the flat-sides of half the shells and top with the remaining shells, pressing them together gently.

Place the white shells in two rows and spread the flat-sides of half the shells with Buttercream. Put a raspberry in the centre of each one and cover with another drop of Buttercream. Top with the remaining shells, pressing them together gently.

Chill the macarons for 12 hours before serving.

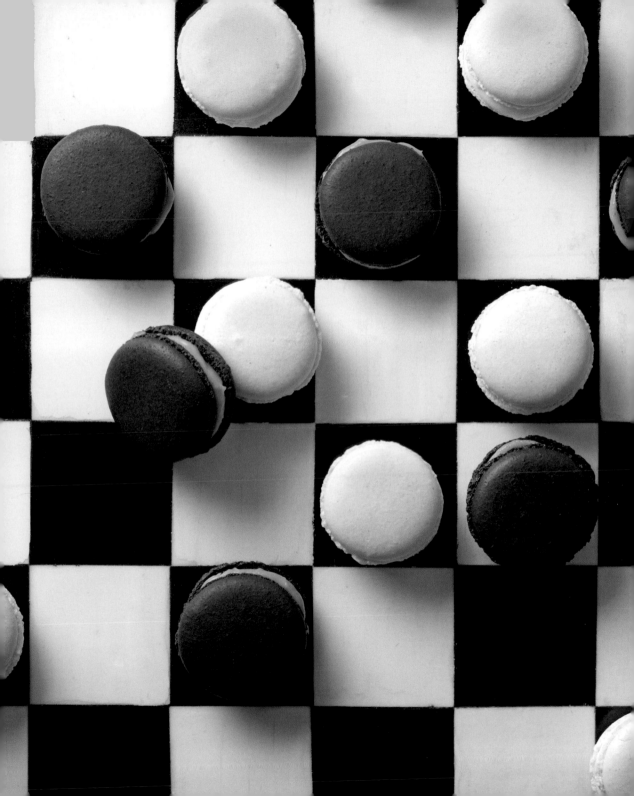

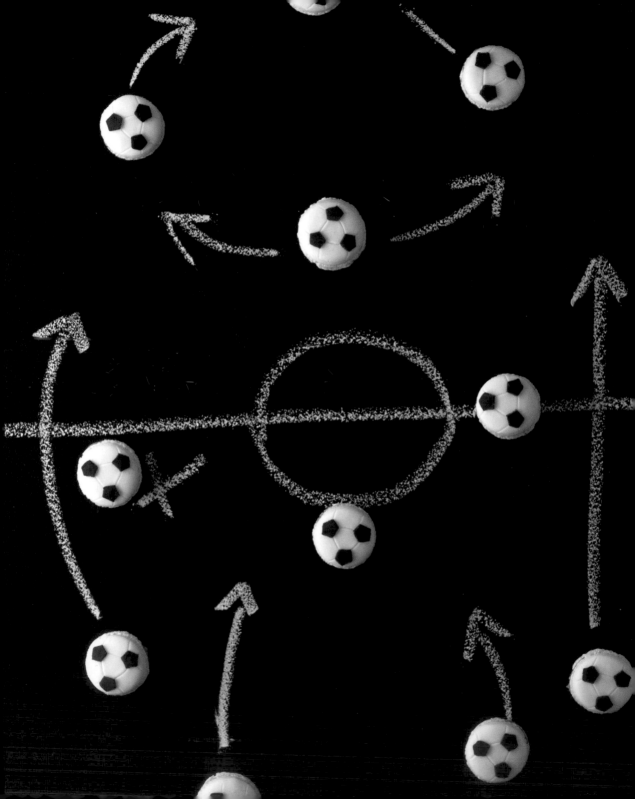

Soccer balls

Little macarons that will be instantly familiar – fans of one of the world's most popular games will be entranced. These sporty treats mean that soccer will be re-enacted on your tabletop.

SHELLS
1 quantity Patissier's Macarons (see page 10)

FILLING
200 g/scant 1 cup chocolate hazelnut spread, such as Nutella

DECORATION
30 g/1 oz. white sugarpaste
10 g/⅓ oz. black sugarpaste
black food colouring

piping bag fitted with a 1-cm/½-inch round tip
4-cm/1½-inch round template (see page 140)
transparent silicone mat
piping bag fitted with a 2-mm/¹⁄₁₆-inch round tip
5-cm/2-inch round cutter
bamboo stick

MAKES 40

Preheat the oven to 160°C (325°F) Gas 3.

Prepare the Patissier's Macarons mixture according to the recipe on page 10. Put the mixture into a piping bag fitted with a 1-cm/½-inch round tip.

Place the 4-cm/1½-inch round template on a baking sheet, and place a silicone mat on top. Pipe 80 round macarons onto the silicone mat, using the template as a guide. (You may need more than one baking sheet.)

Tap the bottom of the sheet lightly on the work surface. Carefully slide the template out from under the mat. Leave the macarons to rest for 15–30 minutes.

Bake the macarons, one sheet at a time, in the preheated oven for 8 minutes, until the tops are crisp and the undersides are dry. Leave to cool for 30 minutes on the baking sheet.

Place the macaron shells in two rows. Spread the chocolate hazelnut spread onto the flat-sides of half the shells and top with the remaining shells, pressing them together gently. Leave to set in the fridge for at least 12 hours before serving.

Knead the white sugarpaste until evenly mixed. Roll out the paste onto a silicone mat and cut circles with the 5-cm/2-inch round cutter. While it is soft, mould the sugarpaste over each macaron. Use a bamboo stick to draw lines in it in a typical football/soccer ball pattern.

Knead the black sugarpaste, roll thinly and cut small dots to resemble the black patches on a soccer ball. Stick the black patches onto the white sugarpaste with a little water. Leave to dry for 1 hour before serving.

Super Bowl

Rustle up these macarons for enthusiasts of American football of all ages and make them part of your celebrations. With three delicious fillings, there is something for everyone in the family to enjoy.

SHELLS
1 quantity Patissier's Macarons (see page 10)
4 g/¾ teaspoon dark brown food colouring

FILLING
1 quantity Dark Chocolate Ganache (see page 30)
1 quantity Caramel Chocolate Ganache (see page 29)
1 quantity Buttercream (see page 27)

DECORATION
1 quantity Royal Icing (see page 20)
black food colouring

piping bag fitted with a 6-mm/¼-inch round tip
Rugby Ball template (see page 141)
transparent silicone mat
small piping bag for icing (decoration)

MAKES 30

Preheat the oven to 160°C (325°F) Gas 3.

Prepare the Patissier's Macarons mixture according to the recipe on page 10, but add the dark brown food colouring before before folding the egg whites into the dry ingredients. Put the mixture into a piping bag fitted with a 6-mm/¼-inch round tip.

Place the Rugby Ball template on a baking sheet, and place a silicone mat on top. Pipe the outline of the Rugby Ball onto the silicone mat, using the template as a guide. Fill in carefully with the macaron mixture and repeat to make 60 ball shapes. (You may need more than one baking sheet.)

Tap the bottom of the sheets lightly on the work surface. Slide the template out from under the mat. Leave the macarons to rest for 15–30 minutes.

Bake the macarons, one sheet at a time, in the preheated oven for 8 minutes, until the tops are crisp and the undersides are dry. Leave to cool for 30 minutes on the baking sheet.

For the filling, spread the Caramel Chocolate Ganache onto the flat-sides of 10 macaron shells, spread the Dark Chocolate Ganache onto the flat-sides of 10 macaron shells and spread the Buttercream onto the flat-sides of 10 macaron shells. Top with the remaining shells, pressing them together gently. Leave to set in the fridge for at least 12 hours before serving.

Prepare the Royal Icing according to the recipe on page 20. Use a toothpick to add a little of the black food colouring to the icing and mix well. Transfer to a small piping bag for icing, and snip off the end to create a small hole. Pipe the lacing lines as shown in the picture on each of the rugby balls. Leave to dry for 1 hour before serving.

Macaron pops

These swirly macaron pops are a lovely idea and are popular with children and adults alike. These have a deliciously chocolate and red berry filling. Do make sure your sticks are suitable for food use.

SHELLS

3 quantities Patissier's Macarons (see page 10)
3 g/²⁄₃ teaspoon lime green food colouring
5 g/1 teaspoon Christmas red food colouring

FILLINGS

2 quantities Dark Chocolate Ganache (see page 30)
100 g dried red berries

2 piping bags fitted with 1-cm/½-inch round tips
7-cm/2¾-inch round template (see page 140)
transparent silicone mat
14 lollipop sticks

MAKES 14

Prepare the first quantity of Patissier's Macarons mixture according to the recipe on page 10. No food colouring is added to this batch.

Prepare the second quantity of Patissier's Macarons mixture according to the recipe on page 10, but add the lime green food colouring before folding the egg whites into the dry ingredients.

Prepare the third quantity of Patissier's Macarons mixture according to the recipe on page 10, but add the Christmas red food colouring before folding the egg whites into the dry ingredients.

Put half of the white macaron mixture down one side of a piping bag fitted with a 1-cm/½-inch round tip, then add the green mixture down the other side of the bag, so that you will get a bit of both colours when piped.

Fill the second piping bag as above, but with the remaining white mixture and the lime green mixture.

Place the 7-cm/2¾-inch round template on a baking sheet, and place a silicone mat on top. Starting from the outside, and leaving 1-mm/¹⁄₁₆-inch between the lines to allow for expansion, pipe 14 green spirals and 14 red spirals within the round templates. (You will need more than one baking sheet.) Tap the bottom of the sheets lightly on the work surface. Slide the template out from under the mat. Leave the macarons to rest for 15–30 minutes.

Bake the macarons, one sheet at a time, in the preheated oven for 12 minutes, until the tops are crisp and the undersides are dry. Leave to cool for 30 minutes on the baking sheet.

To make the filling, prepare the Dark Chocolate Ganache and mix in the dried red berries. Line the macaron shells in pairs of the same colour, flat-side up. Using a teaspoon, place a little Dark Chocolate Ganache mixture onto the macaron shells, add a lollipop stick, then sandwich the pairs together gently. Leave to set in the fridge for at least 12 hours before serving.

You say tomato

These sweet tomatoes are filled with a delicious onion marmalade and buttercream. Bake them in different sizes and you could even try adding some green or orange tomatoes to your crop, if you like.

SHELLS
1 quantity Patissier's
   Macarons (see page 10)
5 g/1 teaspoon cherry red
   food colouring

FILLING
1 quantity Buttercream
   (see page 27)
3 tablespoons onion
   marmalade

DECORATION
30 g/1 oz sugarpaste
2.5 g/½ teaspoon holly
   green food colouring

piping bag fitted with a
   1-cm/½-inch round tip
5-cm/2-inch round template
   (see page 140)
transparent silicone mat
4-cm/1½-inch round
   template (see page 140)
2.5-cm/1-inch round
   template (see page 140)
piping bag fitted with a
   4-mm/⅛-inch round tip

MAKES 30

Preheat the oven to 160°C (325°F) Gas 3.

Prepare the Patissier's Macarons mixture according to the recipe on page 10, but add the cherry red food colouring before folding the egg whites into the dry ingredients. Put the mixture into a piping bag fitted with a 1-cm/½-inch round tip.

Place the 5-cm/2-inch round template on a baking sheet, and place a silicone mat on top. Pipe 20 rounds, using the template as a guide.

Place the 4-cm/1½-inch round template on a baking sheet, and place a silicone mat on top. Pipe 20 rounds, using the template as a guide.

Place the 2.5-cm/1-inch round template on a baking sheet, and place a silicone mat on top. Pipe 20 rounds, using the template as a guide.

Tap the bottom of the sheets lightly on the work surface. Carefully slide the template out from under the mat. Leave the macarons to rest for 15–30 minutes.

Bake the macarons, one sheet at a time, in the preheated oven, until the tops are crisp and the undersides are dry. The 5-cm/2-inch macarons will need 8 minutes, the 4-cm/1½-inch macarons will need 7 minutes, and the 2.5-cm/1-inch macarons will need 6 minutes.

Line the macarons into rows of two in their respective sizes, flat-side up. Put the Buttercream into a piping bag fitted with a 4-mm/⅛-in tip.

Place a small blob of onion marmalade onto the base of one macaron in each pair. Pipe a thin layer of Buttercream round the edge of the onion marmalade, then sandwich the pairs together gently. Leave to set in the fridge for at least 12 hours before serving.

Knead the green food colouring into the white sugarpaste until it is evenly mixed. Use to make green stalks for the tomatoes, and stick one on top of each macaron. Leave to dry for 1 hour before serving.

Sliders

These realistic macaron burger buns are a bit of a departure from the usual sweet treats. They can also be filled with cream cheese and smoked salmon – serve them as a canapé with drinks.

SHELLS
1 quantity Patissier's Macarons (see page 10)
20 g/¾ oz. sesame seeds

FILLING
2 small tomatoes, cut into 25 slices, ideally about the same size as your macarons
25 small pieces of soft lettuce
25 x 7.5 cm/2-inch cheese slices

piping bag fitted with a 1-cm/½-inch round tip
6-cm/2⅜-inch round template (see page 140)
transparent silicone mat

MAKES 25

Preheat the oven to 160°C (325°F) Gas 3.

Prepare the Patissier's Macarons mixture according to the recipe on page 10, adding no food colouring. Put the mixture into a piping bag fitted with a 1-cm/½-inch round tip.

Place the 6-cm/2⅜-inch round template on a baking sheet, and place a silicone mat on top. Pipe 50 rounds, using the template as a guide. (You will need more than one baking sheet.)

Tap the bottom of the sheets lightly on the work surface. Sprinkle the sesame seeds on top. Slide the template out from under the mat. Leave the macarons to rest for 15–30 minutes.

Bake the macarons, one sheet at a time, in the preheated oven for 10 minutes until the tops are crisp and the undersides are dry.

Lay cheese slices on half of the macaron shells, then add the lettuce slices and, lastly, the tomato. Top with another macaron shell.

Serve as soon as possible as the fillings will quickly make them soft and unappetizing.

Seasonal Celebrations

Chinese lanterns

Chinese New Year is a great chance for a beautiful feast of vibrant colour in the form of these macaron red lanterns.

SHELLS
1 quantity Patissier's Macarons (see page 10)
5 g/1 teaspoon extra red food colouring

FILLING
mandarin conserve
1 quantity Dark Chocolate Ganache (see page 30)

DECORATION
2.5 g/½ teaspoon yellow food colouring
30 g/1 oz. sugarpaste
gold food colouring powder, diluted with a little rejuvenating spirit

piping bag fitted with a 1-cm/½-inch round tip
5.5-cm/2¼-inch round, 4.5-cm/1¾-inch round, 3.5-cm/1⅜-inch round and 2.5-cm/1-inch round templates (see page 140)
transparent silicone mat
small slim paintbrush

MAKES 40

Preheat the oven to 160°C (325°F) Gas 3.

Prepare the Patissier's Macarons mixture according to the recipe on page 10, but add the extra red food colouring before folding the egg whites into the dry ingredients. Put the mixture into a piping bag fitted with a 1-cm/½-inch round tip.

Place the 5.5-cm/2¼-inch round template on a baking sheet, and place a silicone mat on top. Pipe 20 rounds onto the silicone mat, using the template as a guide. Repeat the steps above with the other 3 sizes. (You will need more than one baking sheet.) Tap the bottom of the sheets lightly on the work surface. Slide the template out from under the mat. Leave the macarons to rest for 15–30 minutes.

Bake the macarons, one sheet at a time, in the preheated oven as follows: 5.5-cm/2¼-inch macarons 8 minutes; 4.5-cm/1¾-inch macarons 7 minutes; 3.5-cm/1⅜-inch macarons 6 minutes; 2.5-cm/1-inch macarons 4 minutes, until the tops are crisp and the undersides are dry. Leave to cool for 30 minutes on the baking sheets.

To fill, mix 2–3 tablespoons of mandarin conserve into the Dark Chocolate Ganache. Spread a teaspoonful of the filling onto the flat-side of half of the macarons, and top with a macaron of matching size, pressing them together gently. Leave to set in the fridge for at least 12 hours before finishing.

Add the yellow food colouring to the white sugarpaste. Knead until the colour is even, then roll out to a thickness of 3 mm/⅛ inch Shape into half-moons in four different sizes to make the tops and bottoms of the lanterns. Stick the soft sugarpaste to the tops and bases of the macarons and paint gold lines on the lanterns. Leave to dry for 1 hour.

Cherry blossom

The delicate beauty of Japanese cherry blossom season is captured in these divine macarons. They are filled with a sakura-scented buttercream and hand-painted with branches of flowers.

SHELLS
1 quantity Patissier's
  Macarons (see page 10)
3 g/⅔ teaspoon dusky
  pink food colouring

FILLING
1 quantity Buttercream
  (see page 27)
edible sakura paste or
  other edible flower
  paste, to taste

DECORATION
2.5 g/½ teaspoon brown
  food colouring
2.5 g/½ teaspoon pink
  food colouring
2.5 g/½ teaspoon white
  food colouring

*piping bag fitted with a
  1-cm/½-inch round tip*
*5-cm/2-inch round template
  (see page 140)*
transparent silicone mat
fine paintbrush

MAKES 40

Preheat the oven to 160°C (325°F) Gas 3.

Prepare the Patissier's Macarons mixture according to the recipe on page 10, but add the dusky pink food colouring before folding the egg whites into the dry ingredients. Put the mixture into a piping bag fitted with a 1-cm/½-inch round tip.

Place the 5-cm/2-inch round template on a baking sheet, and place a silicone mat on top. Pipe 80 rounds, using the template as a guide. (You will need more than one baking sheet.) Tap the bottom of the sheets lightly on the work surface. Slide the template out from under the mat. Leave the macarons to rest for 15–30 minutes.

Bake the macarons, one sheet at a time, in the preheated oven for 8 minutes, until the tops are crisp and the undersides are dry. Leave to cool for 30 minutes on the baking sheet.

To fill, mix the edible sakura flower petals into the Buttercream.

Spread a teaspoonful of the filling mixture onto the flat-sides of half of the shells, and top with the remaining macaron shells, pressing together gently. Leave to set in the fridge for at least 12 hours before finishing.

Prepare the food colouring paints according to the packet instructions, and use a clean, fine paintbrush to paint branches of cherry blossom onto the tops of the macarons. Leave to dry for 1 hour before serving.

Spring chicks

Children of all ages will delight in this flock of chirpy chicks. There's no need to limit them to Easter – they would make a welcome addition to party fare at any time of the year.

SHELLS
**1 quantity Patissier's
    Macarons (see page 10)**
**3 g/⅔ teaspoon melon
    food colouring**

DECORATION
**1 quantity Royal Icing
    (see page 20)**
black food colouring
orange food colouring

*piping bag fitted with a
    1-cm/½-inch round tip*
*Easter Chicks template
    (see page 141)*
transparent silicone mat
*2 small piping bags for
    icing*

MAKES 60

Preheat the oven to 160°C (325°F) Gas 3.

Prepare the Patissier's Macarons mixture according to the recipe on page 10, but add the melon food colouring before folding the egg whites into the dry ingredients. Put the mixture into a piping bag fitted with a 1-cm/½-inch round tip.

Place the chicks template on a baking sheet, and place a silicone mat on top. Pipe 60 chicks, using the template as a guide: start with a round head, then pipe a slightly larger round body, and drag the tail with a flick. (You will need more than one baking sheet.)

Tap the bottom of the sheet lightly on the work surface. Slide the template out from under the mat. Leave the macarons to rest for 15–30 minutes.

Bake the macarons, one sheet at a time, in the preheated oven for 8 minutes, until the tops are crisp and the undersides are dry. Leave to cool for 30 minutes on the baking sheet.

Make the Royal Icing recipe and, using a toothpick, add enough black food colouring to create a dark shade for the eyes to about a third of the mixture. Transfer to one of the small piping bags. Snip off the end to create a small hole and pipe an eye onto each chick.

In the same way, add the orange food colouring to the remaining Royal Icing, transfer to the other piping bag and pipe on the beaks and a few feathers. Leave to dry for 1 hour before serving.

Swedish midsummer flowers

In Sweden, midsummer celebrations involve people wearing
a flower wreath in their hair and dressing a maypole with blooms.

SHELLS

**5 quantities Patissier's
Macarons (see page 10)**

**3 g/²⁄₃ teaspoon each of
primrose and lavender
food colouring**

**5 g/1 teaspoon each of
Egyptian orange and
rose pink food
colouring**

**3.5 g/²⁄₃ teaspoon royal
blue food colouring**

FILLING

**2 quantities Buttercream
(see page 27)**

4–6 drops rose essence

DECORATION

20 g/¾ oz. sugarpaste

**1 quantity Royal Icing
(see page 20)**

**2.5 g/½ teaspoon orange
food colouring**

*5 piping bags fitted with
6-mm/¼-inch round tips*
*flower template (see
page 141)*
transparent silicone mat
small piping bag for icing
tiny flower cutter

MAKES 35 OF EACH

Preheat the oven to 160°C (325°F) Gas 3.

Prepare the first Patissier's Macaron quantity according to the
recipe on page 10, but add the lavender food colouring before folding
the egg whites into the dry ingredients. Put the mixture into a piping
bag fitted with a 6-mm/¼-inch round tip.

Place the Flower template on a baking sheet, and place a silicone
mat on top. Using the template as a guide, start piping from the outer
edge of the petals and gently pull inwards to fill in the flower. Repeat
to make 70 flowers. (You may need more than one baking sheet.) Tap
the bottom of the sheets lightly on the work surface. Slide the template
out from under the mat. Leave the macarons to rest for 15–30 minutes.

Bake the macarons, one sheet at a time, in the preheated oven for
10 minutes, until the tops are crisp and the undersides are dry. Leave
to cool for 30 minutes on the baking sheet.

Meanwhile, prepare and bake the remaining 4 quantities of
Patissier's Macarons in the same way, using the yellow, orange, red
and blue food colourings for each separate quantity of flowers.

To fill, mix the Buttercream with the rose essence. Spread a
teaspoonful of the filling mixture onto the flat-sides of half of the
shells, and top with the remaining macaron shells, pressing together
gently. Make sure that all the petals align. Leave to set in the fridge
for at least 12 hours before finishing.

Knead the sugarpaste until softened. Roll it out and use a tiny
flower cutter to cut about 175 flowers.

Add the orange food colouring to the Royal Icing, mixing well.
Fill the small piping bag for icing and pipe tiny dots in the middle
of the flowers. Use the rest of the icing to stick the flowers onto the
centre of the macarons. Leave to dry for 1 hour before serving.

Firework fiesta

Whether you are welcoming in the New Year, celebrating the 4th of July or having a bonfire party, fireworks help the event go with a bang. These edible versions have a paprika-kick of their own.

SHELLS
2 quantities Patissier's Macarons (see page 10)
5 g/1 teaspoon extra black food colouring

FILLING
hot paprika, to taste
1 quantity Dark Chocolate Ganache (see page 30)

DECORATION
1 quantity Royal Icing (see page 20)
5 g/1 teaspoon yellow food colouring
5 g/1 teaspoon Egyptian orange food colouring
5 g/1 teaspoon fuchsia pink food colouring
5 g/1 teaspoon royal blue food colouring

piping bag fitted with a 1-cm/½-inch round tip
5-cm/2-inch round template (see page 140)
transparent silicone mat
4 small piping bags for icing

MAKES 40

Preheat the oven to 160°C (325°F) Gas 3.

Prepare the first quantity of Patissier's Macarons mixture according to the recipe on page 10, but add the extra black food colouring before folding the egg whites into the dry ingredients. Put the mixture into a piping bag fitted with a 1-cm/½-inch round tip.

Place the 5-cm/2 inch round template on a baking sheet, and place a silicone mat on top. Pipe 80 macarons, using the template as a guide. (You will need more than one baking sheet.) Tap the bottom of the sheets lightly on the work surface. Slide the template out from under the mat. Leave the macarons to rest for 15–30 minutes.

Bake the macarons, one sheet at a time, in the preheated oven for 8 minutes, until the tops are crisp and the undersides are dry. Leave to cool for 30 minutes on the baking sheet.

To fill, mix paprika into the Dark Chocolate Ganache, to taste. Using a teaspoon, place a little of the chocolate filling mixture onto half of the shells, and sandwich the pairs together gently. Leave to set in the fridge for at least 12 hours before finishing.

Divide the Royal Icing into four portions. Add each of the food colourings to one of the portions and knead until the colour is even. Transfer each to a small piping bag and snip off the ends to create small holes. Draw lines of firework sparklers on each of the macarons. Leave to dry for 1 hour before serving.

Spooky spiders

Make a batch of these deliciously spine-chilling spiders for a Halloween party and watch your guests try to decide whether to scream and run, or brave it out and gobble one up!

SHELLS
1 quantity Patissier's Macarons (see page 10)
5 g/1 teaspoon extra black food colouring

FILLING
100 g/3½ oz. ready-made marshmallow fluff

DECORATION
30 g/1 oz. white sugarpaste/fondant
black food colouring
1 quantity Royal Icing (see page 20)

piping bag fitted with a 1-cm/½-inch round tip
5-cm/2-inch round template (see page 140)
transparent silicone mat
2 small piping bags for icing

MAKES 40 SPIDERS

Preheat the oven to 160°C (325°F) Gas 3.

Prepare the Patissier's Macarons mixture according to the recipe on page 10, but add the extra black food colouring before folding the egg whites into the dry ingredients. Put the mixture into a piping bag fitted with a 1-cm/½-inch round tip.

Place the 5-cm/2 inch round template on a baking sheet, and place a silicone mat on top. Pipe 80 macarons, using the template as a guide. (You will need more than one baking sheet.) Tap the bottom of the sheets lightly on the work surface. Slide the template out from under the mat. Leave the macarons to rest for 15–30 minutes.

Bake the macarons, one sheet at a time, in the preheated oven for 8 minutes, until the tops are crisp and the undersides are dry. Leave to cool for 30 minutes on the baking sheet.

To fill, using a teaspoon, place a little marshmallow fluff onto half of the shells, and sandwich the pairs together gently to create 40 macaron spider bodies. Decorate immediately.

Use a toothpick to add some black food colouring to the white sugarpaste. Knead until the colour is even. Make the legs by rolling the paste out into long thin sausages. Cut the lengths to make 8 for each spider. Use the filling to attach the legs in between the macaron shells.

Next, make the Royal Icing and divide it into two portions. Transfer one portion to a small piping bag and snip off the end to create a small hole. Pipe 8 white eyes on the top of each spider.

Use a toothpick to add enough black food colouring to the other portion to create a dark shade. Transfer to the other small piping bag and snip off the end to create a small hole. Pipe eyeballs on the top of each white eye. Leave to dry for 1 hour before serving.

Frosty snowmen

These jolly snowmen, filled with a rich candied chestnut cream, will be a hit at Christmas. Make them when the weather is cold outside and serve with warming mugs of hot chocolate.

SHELLS
1 quantity Patissier's Macarons (see page 10)

FILLING
50 g/2 oz. candied chestnuts
1 quantity Buttercream (see page 27)

DECORATION
1 quantity Royal Icing (see page 20)
black food colouring
tangerine food colouring
holly green food colouring
royal blue food colouring
Christmas red food colouring

icing/confectioners' sugar, for dusting
piping bag fitted with a 1-cm/½-inch round tip
Snowman template (see page 141)
transparent silicone mat
5 small piping bags for icing

MAKES 25

Preheat the oven to 160°C (325°F) Gas 3.

Prepare the Patissier's Macarons mixture according to the recipe on page 10. Put the mixture into the piping bag fitted with a 1-cm/½-inch round tip.

Place the Snowman template on a baking sheet, and place a silicone mat on top. Using the template as a guide, pipe a snowman on to the silicone mat. Start at the top of the head then follow with the body. Repeat to make 25 snowmen (you will need more than one baking sheet).

Tap the bottom of the sheets lightly on the work surface. Slide the template out from under the mat. Leave the macarons to rest for 20–40 minutes.

Bake the macarons, one sheet at a time, in the preheated oven for 12 minutes, until the tops are crisp and the undersides are dry. Leave to cool for 30 minutes on the baking sheets.

To fill, finely chop the candied chestnuts and mix them with the Buttercream. Line the snowmen macarons into rows of 2, flat-side up. Using a teaspoon, place a little chestnut filling mixture onto half of the shells, and sandwich the pairs together gently to create 25 macarons. Leave to set in the fridge for at least 12 hours before finishing.

Prepare the Royal Icing recipe, then divide it equally into 5 portions. Use a toothpick to add a little of each food colouring to each portion and mix. Transfer the black to a small piping bag for icing, and snip off the end to create a small hole.

Pipe the eyes and buttons in black, then repeat with the tangerine in a second piping bag and give the snowmen carrot noses. Use the remaining three colours for the snowmen's scarves. Leave to dry for 1 hour, then lightly dust the macarons with icing/confectioners' sugar before serving.

Merry & bright baubles

These edible baubles make a perfect festive gift. Make them in your preferred colours and decorate them however you fancy with coloured sugarpastes in stamped out in Christmas/holiday designs.

SHELLS

4 quantities Patissier's Macarons (see page 10)

4 g/¾ teaspoon your choice of food colouring for each batch

FILLING

1 quantity Dark Chocolate Ganache (see page 30)

120 g/4 oz honeycomb/ sponge candy, crushed

1 quantity White Chocolate Ganache (see page 31)

a few drops peppermint essence oil, to taste

DECORATION

1 quantity Royal Icing (see page 20)

sugarpaste in assorted colours

4.5-cm/1¾-inch round template (see page 140)

transparent silicone mat

4 piping bags fitted with 6-mm/¼-round tips

1 small piping bag for icing

assorted Christmas cutters

MAKES 160

Preheat the oven to 160°C (325°F) Gas 3.

Prepare the first quantity of Patissier's Macarons mixture according to the recipe on page 10, but add your first chosen food colouring before folding the egg whites into the dry ingredients. Put the mixture into a piping bag fitted with a 6-mm/¼-inch round tip.

Place the 4.5-cm/1¾-inch round template on a baking sheet, and place a silicone mat on top. Pipe 80 rounds onto the silicone mat, using the template as a guide. (You will need more than one baking sheet.) Tap the bottom of the sheets lightly on the work surface. Slide the template out from under the mat. Leave the macarons to rest for 15–30 minutes.

Bake the macarons, one sheet at a time, in the preheated oven for 8 minutes, until the tops are crisp and the undersides are dry. Leave the oven on and allow to cool for 30 minutes on the baking sheets.

Meanwhile, prepare and bake the remaining 3 quantities of Patissier's Macarons in the same way, using one of your chosen food colourings for each separate batch.

To make the fillings, mix the Dark Chocolate Ganache with the crushed honeycomb and mix the White Chocolate Ganache with the peppermint oil. Line the macarons up in pair, flat-side up. Using a teaspoon, place a little of the Dark Chocolate filling onto half of the shells and the White Chocolate mixture on to the remaining and sandwich the pairs together gently. Leave to set in the fridge for at least 12 hours before finishing.

Make the Royal Icing recipe, cover, and keep aside to use to stick the sugarpaste decorations on to the macarons. Roll out your various coloured sugarpastes to a thickness of 3 mm/⅛ inch and use the cookie cutters to stamp out 20 small Christmas shapes and use the trimmings to create any details. Use a little of the Royal Icing to stick them onto the macaron shells. Leave to dry for 1 hour before serving.

Templates

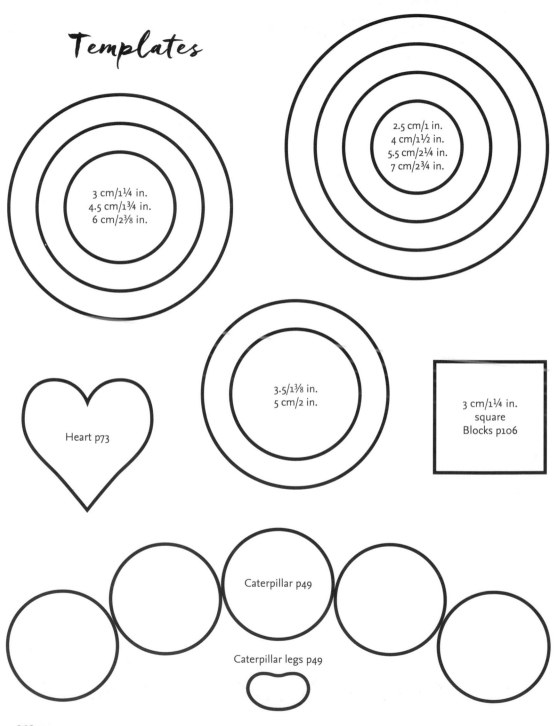

2.5 cm/1 in.
4 cm/1½ in.
5.5 cm/2¼ in.
7 cm/2¾ in.

3 cm/1¼ in.
4.5 cm/1¾ in.
6 cm/2⅜ in.

3.5/1⅜ in.
5 cm/2 in.

3 cm/1¼ in.
square
Blocks p106

Heart p73

Caterpillar p49

Caterpillar legs p49

Chicks p107

Rugby ball p133

Snowman p116

Flower p136

Tetris p126

Index